365 WAYS TO GET YOUR CHILD TO SLEEP

Paula Elbirt, M.D.
with Linda Lee Small

Adams Media Corporation
Holbrook, Massachusetts

Copyright ©2001, Paula Elbirt-Bender and Linda Lee Small. All rights reserved. This book, or parts thereof, may not be reproduced in any form without permission from the publisher; exceptions are made for brief excerpts used in published reviews.

Published by Adams Media Corporation
260 Center Street, Holbrook, MA 02343
www.adamsmedia.com

ISBN: 1-58062-384-0

Printed in Canada.

J I H G F E D C B A

Library of Congress Cataloging-in-Publication Data
365 ways to get your child to sleep /
Paula Elbirt and Linda Lee Small
p. cm,
ISBN 1-58062-384-0
1. Sleep disorders in children. 2. Infants--Sleep. 3. Children--Sleep.
I. Title: Three hundred sixty-five ways to get your child to sleep. II. Small, Linda Lee. III. Title.
RJ506.S55 E2   2001
618.92'8498--dc21   2001022399

Many of the designations used by manufacturers and sellers to distinguish their products are claimed as trademarks. Where those designations appear in this book and Adams Media was aware of a trademark claim, the designations have been printed in initial capital letters.

This publication is designed to provide accurate and authoritative information with regard to the subject mattered covered. It is sold with the understanding that the publisher is not engaged in rendering professional medical advice. If assistance is required, the servicesof a competent professional should be sought.

Illustrations by Barry Littmann.
Cover photo by Mitch Diamond/International Stock

This book is available at quantity discounts for bulk purchases.
For information, call 1-800-872-5627.

Contents
0-3 Months: Newborns

1. Do not take your baby's sleep habits personally

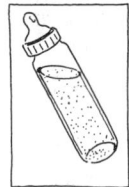
2. Don't fill up baby on cereal

3. Myth: If a breastfeeding mother drinks wine...

4. Breastfed babies versus bottle-fed babies

5. Put baby on his back

6. Swaddling

7. Ventilate the crib

8. Sleep whenever the baby sleeps

9. Don't let the baby fall asleep on you

10. Don't let baby sleep with a bottle

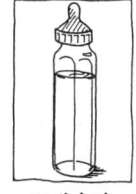
11. No bottle, continued: Feed baby <u>before</u> bed

12. Not all cribs are created equal

365 WAYS TO GET YOUR CHILD TO SLEEP

13. Overlying

14. Correct sleep attire (newborns)

15. Myth: "Did you hear the one about the cat...?"

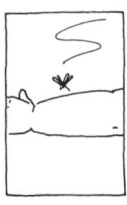
16. Mosquito netting

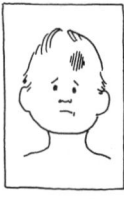
17. Cranial molding (AKA flat head)

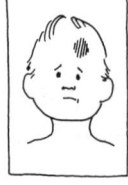
18. Flat head, continued

19. Just say no... to soft surfaces

20. Just say no... to sheepskin

21. Close to you

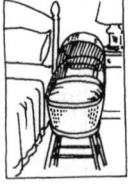
22. The first six weeks

23. The safe bassinet

24. The mattress

25. Sheets

26. Just say no... to pillows

27. Be careful of makeshift sleeping areas

28. Go on night patrol for safety

29. Let baby fall asleep in his crib

30. The last thing that a baby remembers

31. Transferring baby

32. Babies like to suck...pacifiers

33. Hostage to the pacifier?

34. "Stimulate" your baby to sleep

35. Music soothes— Sing

36. Be a one-parent band

37. Stuffed animals with a beat

38. Transitional objects, part I

39. Napping

40. Catnaps: On <u>your</u> belly

41. Catnaps: Try a Snugli

42. Catnaps: Swing time

43. Keep a sleep diary

44. Cozy napping place

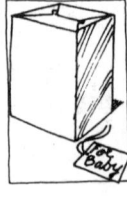

45. The Nikken

46. Just say no... to a newborn crying in her crib

47. The two-hour rule

48. FYI: How much sleep does a baby need?

49. Never wake a sleeping baby unless...

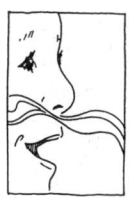
50. Aromatherapy

51. Use a wedge system

52. Use a halo to snuggle her head

53. Put a hat on her head

54. Nature's Cradle

55. Jiggle the bassinet

56. Go for a car ride

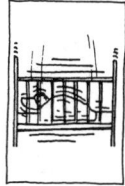
57. Attach a mechanical crib jiggler

58. Drifting lullabies

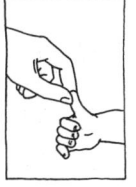
59. Babies like to suck...fingers

60. Quiet down the environment

 61. Wake a sleeping baby for dinner

 62. Hum tunelessly

 63. Cozy warmed mitten and booties

 64. Nip sleep problems in the bud

 65. Teaching day versus night

 66. More on day/night confusion

 67. The six-week miracle

 68. Understanding colic

 69. Colic and sleep

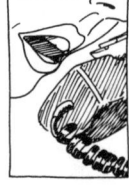 70. Perception is everything

 71. Count "feeding" as sleeping time

 72. Don't let an infant cry herself to sleep

 73. Keep baby's arm down

 74. Positional molding

 75. Just say yes... to intercoms

 76. Just say no... to intercoms

 77. Be a little flexible (but let the mattress be firm)

 78. Laying on of hands

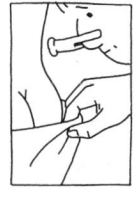 79. Crying baby: Check diaper if baby won't sleep

 80. The miracle reflex

 81. Expect to rise to the occasion

3–12 Months: Infants

82. Put the car seat into the crib

83. Play dead

84. Safe sleep position

85. Naptime: Cradle

86. Naptime: Infant rocking seat

87. Naptime: Stroller, outdoors

88. Naptime: Stroller, indoors

89. Jogging with sleeping baby

90. Infants and napping

91. Change in sleeping patterns

92. "It's bedtime"

93. Climate Control

94. Do the ritual over and over again

95. When the ritual is over

96. Rituals: Both parents take part

97. Side sleeping

98. Do a safety check

99. Less is best

100. The five-minute rule

101. Middle of the night

102. Put a piece of your clothing into the crib

103. Do not rock baby to sleep in your arms

104. White noise

105. Never wake a baby <u>except</u> when he is asleep in the car

106. Does baby need a humidifier?

107. Watch for signs of sleepiness

108. Put infant on a machine that vibrates

109. Rocking chair

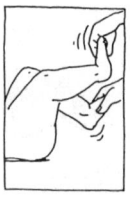
110. Massage baby's feet

111. Song: "Over the Meadow"

112. Play Enya

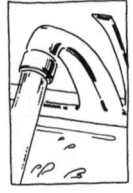
113. Take a bath for two

114. Play a metronome

115. Warm the sheets in a dryer

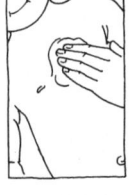
116. Find the sleep trigger spots

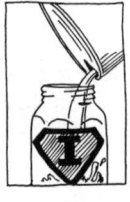
117. Crying baby: Is her formula too strong?

118. Close your eyes

119. Yawn a lot

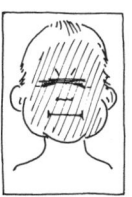
120. Sleep-time for children with asthma and allergies

121. Is it health related?

122. If a parent comes home late, don't wake baby up

123. Reinforce sleep training

124. Tolerate noise

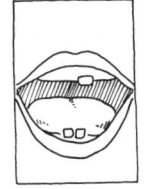
125. Teething

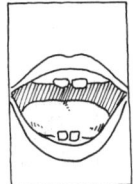
126. Teething, part II

127. Sing "Good Night Irene"

128. Read or sing Lullaby and Goodnight: Songs for...

129. Sing "Hush Little Baby"

 130. Don't run in too soon

 131. Just say no... to water beds

 132. Stick to your bedtime

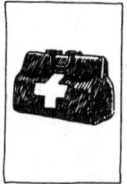 133. All bets are off if your infant is sick

 134. Question: Why is it that the later my baby goes to bed...

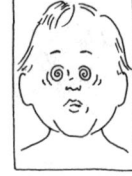 135. What's a good bedtime?

 136. Wake-up time

 137. Head banging

 138. Massage

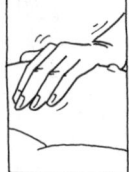 139. Massage, part II

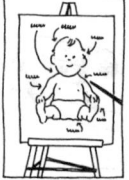 140. Tips for international adoption

 141. Adoption continued: Does baby need company?

142. Adoption continued: Sing lullaby...

143. Infants and traveling

144. Daylight savings time

145. Treating baby's cold

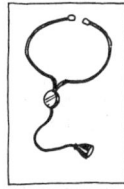

146. Colds continued: Elevate baby

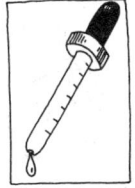

147. Just say no... to cold medicines

148. Treating baby's gas

149. Just say no... to simethicone

150. The medicine cabinet for infants

151. Sing "Alice the Camel"

152. Be prepared

153. Blackout shades

154. Family bed

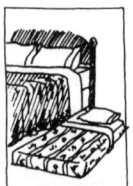

155. Sleeping arrangements: "Sidecar"

156. Safe sleep position, revisited

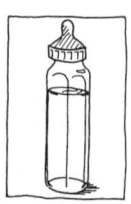

157. Wean baby from early morning feedings

158. Desperate measures: Nurse until you both fall asleep

159. Sing "Keemo Kymo"

160. Avoid caffeine

161. Tea time

162. Sleeping arrangements: The extended bed

163. Identical twins

164. Fraternal twins

165. Simulate a baby's bedroom

 166. Read (or sing) *Sleep, Sleep, Sleep: A Lullaby for Little Ones*

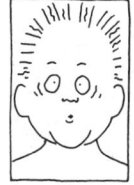 167. Parent-to-parent: The white wall

12–36 Months: Toddlers

168. FYI: Toddlers resist bedtime

169. Don't feed toddler solids close to bedtime

170. Bedroom door open

171. Bedroom door shut

172. Let your child wish on a star

173. Put your children in the same room

174. Toddlers and colds

175. Just say no... to your toddler sleeping with you

176. Enjoy your toddler during the day

177. Bedtime ritual, revisited

178. Toddlers and timers

179. Just say no...to your toddler's being a TV-couch potato

 180. Sleep training: Breaking the crying and waking pattern

 181. The five-minute rule, revisited

 182. Enlist aid of older siblings

 183. No extras

 184. Don't sneak out of your toddler's room

 185. No falling asleep in your bed

 186. Choosing bedtime and wake-up time

 187. Sharing a room: Same bedtime

 188. Sharing a room: Different bedtimes

 189. Parent-to-parent: Whisper

 190. Unwind time

 191. "Stuffed" friends

192. Transitional objects, revisited

193. Don't sneak out

194. "Mommy and Daddy": Getting attention

195. Bedtime problems

196. Crawling out of the crib

197. Time for a real bed

198. The big bed transition

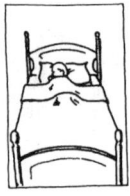
199. Big bed, part II

200. Read <u>My New Bed: From Crib to Bed</u>

201. Leaving bed

202. Rely on sitters with older children

203. "Help, there's a child in my bed"

 204. The parent chair

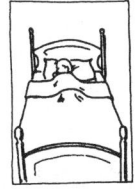 205. During the day, reinforce his need to sleep in his own bed

 206. Play "let's sleep"

 207. Reward the child in the big bed

 208. "Say goodnight to everyone who loves you"

 209. Go on monster patrol

 210. Read <u>The Tooth Fairies' Nighttime Visit</u>

 211. Say prayers

 212. Read <u>Good Night, God Bless</u>

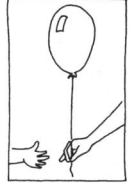 213. Special reward

 214. Limit liquids at bedtime

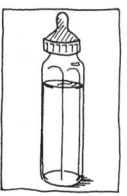 215. Parent-to-parent: Give warm milk

365 WAYS TO GET YOUR CHILD TO SLEEP

 216. Turn over an hourglass

 217. Waking up from napping

 218. Forget logic: Very tired toddlers have trouble sleeping

 219. Let's hear it for night-lights

 220. Brrr!

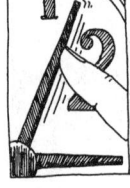 221. Toddler sleep review

 222. "One more, no more"

 223. Nighttime concerns

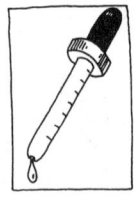 224. Just say no... to sedatives

 225. Concept of time

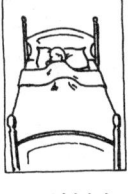 226. Adult beds are for adults

 227. Restless sleepers, part I

228. Restless sleepers, part II

229. Keep to your ritual wherever you are

230. Waking from napping, revisited

231. Reschedule naps

232. Counting sheep

233. The roaming toddler

234. The bedroom

235. FYI: General sleep fact

236. When parents' bedtime styles clash

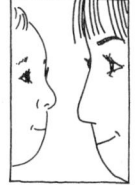
237. "There never was a child so lovely"

238. Sing "Lullaby and Good Night"

239. Sleep log

365 WAYS TO GET YOUR CHILD TO SLEEP

240. Waking a child at naptime

241. Establish an earlier bedtime

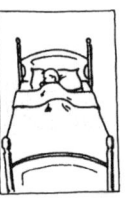
242. Wake-up time

243. Disturbances

244. Yoga breathing

245. "Relax your toes"

246. Prerecord bedtime stories

247. Obstructive sleep apnea (OSA)

248. Read <u>Sleep, Little One, Sleep</u>

249. Toddlers and traveling

250. Rituals for wake-up

251. Wake-up cuddles

252. Family bed: Good morning, world

253. Cold medicine

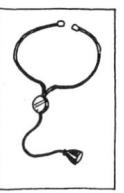
254. Croup: The illness

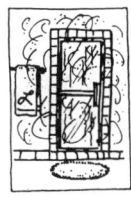
255. Croup: The treatment

256. Final words on croup

257. Earaches

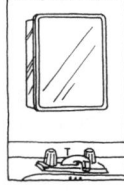
258. The medicine cabinet for toddlers

259. Sunburn

260. Painkillers

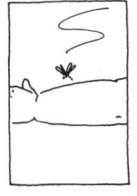
261. Insect bites

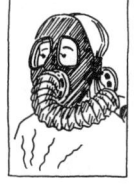
262. Gas

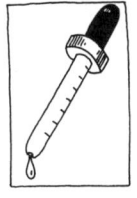
263. "A spoonful of sugar"

365 WAYS TO GET YOUR CHILD TO SLEEP

 264. Vomiting

 265. Pillows, revisited

 266. Just say no... to television

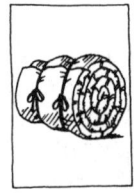 267. The sleeping bag solution

 268. Bedtime snacks

 269. Decongest your house

 270. Sing a Welsh lullaby

 271. Sing an Irish lullaby

 272. Nighttime walks

 273. Read <u>Good Night, Gorilla</u>

 274. Set up an aquarium

 275. Nightmares

276. Calming nightmares

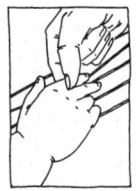
277. Nightmare prevention

278. Night terrors

279. Peeking in on your toddler

280. In some cultures babies <u>are</u> given alcohol

3–6 Years: Preschoolers

281. Reinforce bedtime

282. Set limits

283. Read <u>Can't You Sleep, Little Bear?</u> to dispel fear of the dark

284. Read <u>Goodnight (A Pop-up Lullaby)</u> just for the giggles

285. The early riser

286. Make a dream catcher

287. Prebedtime rules

288. Make sleep a priority "chore," not a punishment

289. Parent-to-parent: Read <u>In the Night Kitchen</u>

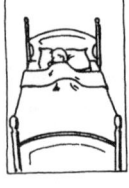

290. Napping

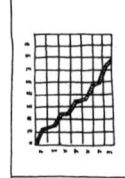

291. Recommended daily sleep allowance

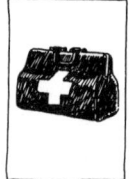

292. Connection between sleep and illness

 293. Create a tent

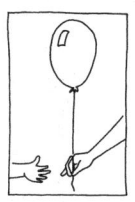 294. Reward cooperation

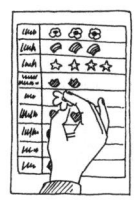 295. Make a bedtime star chart

 296. Connect the reward to bedtime

 297. The 20-minute solution

 298. Sleepwalking

 299. Bunk beds

 300. Add 15 minutes to bedtime storytelling

 301. Sleep talking

 302. Leave wake-up goodies

 303. Read *Goodnight Moon*

 304. Keep an "up" child down

 305. Day affects night

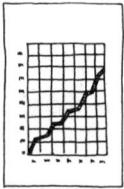 306. Review: Sleep milestones

 307. Thumb sucking, revisited

 308. Prepare for change

 309. Naps, continued

 310. "The sun will come out...tomorrow"

 311. Why? Why? Why?

 312. Sleep instructions

 313. Vacation time

 314. Massage: "My turn"

 315. Children of divorce

 316. "Uh, where do I sleep?"

317. Divorce: Easing into bedtime

318. Divorce: Create a new ritual

319. Travel: Sleep tips

320. Day-Glo stickers for nighttime

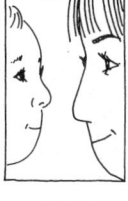
321. Good morning/good-bye

322. The first sleepover

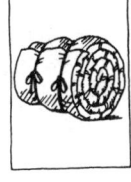
323. Sleepover: Rehearsal

324. Guess who's sleeping over

325. Fever

326. Bed-wetting: The facts

327. Bed-wetting and sleeping

328. The wet bed

329. Bed-wetting: Dressing for success

330. No punishment

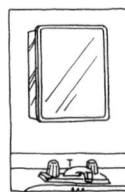
331. The medicine cabinet for preschoolers

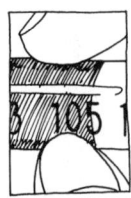
332. Just say no... to a thermometer at night

333. Stuffed animals stand guard!

334. Colds and the preschooler

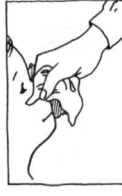
335. Treating a stuffed nose

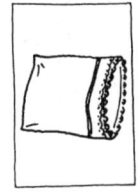
336. Teeth grinding

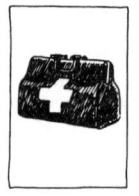
337. Earaches

338. Last words of the evening

339. Never say goodnight in anger

340. Avoid junk foods close to bedtime

341. Parent-to-parent: Rub the third eye

342. Parent-to-parent: Rub eyebrows

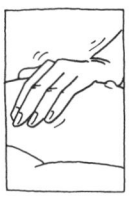

343. Parent-to-parent: Stroke lightly

344. Read <u>I Don't Want to Sleep Tonight</u>

345. Parent-to-parent: Ending a night terror

346. The bedtime pass

347. The night after a vaccine

348. The night after a trauma

349. The hospital experience

350. The magic disc

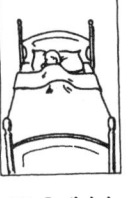

351. Family bed, revisited

352. Just say no... to snoring

353. Read <u>Where the Wild Things Are</u>

354. Hotlines

355. Magazines

356. Web sites

357. Sleep problems

358. Read <u>The Sleep Book for Tired Parents</u>

359. Signs of sleep disorders

360. Sleep-disorder clinics, and more

361. Sing "Waltzing Matilda"

362. Lullabies online

363. Sleep affects behavior

364. Waking up in the middle of the night can be a good sign!

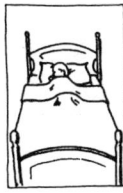

365. The last word

Introduction

Let me share with you the time I threatened to give away my firstborn to a stranger. My son David *never* slept through the night until he was seven months old. My pediatrician had assured me at the three-month checkup that David would magically start to sleep through the night, but that magic moment was a long time coming. I figured that was retribution for *me* telling the parents in my practice to expect their child to sleep through the night at three months.

So David was now seven months old and we were on vacation—you could say he was "Sleepless in San Diego." My husband and I were stuck in a hotel room with a baby who was operating on New York time and shrieking his little lungs out. We decided to take a trip and drive somewhere—anywhere—because babies love car rides (see tip # 56). Since David didn't seem to understand this rule either, we just kept on driving until we were in Tijuana. It was now morning and people were coming out into the street and selling their wares—sombreros, piñatas, hand-woven blankets.

I spied a lovely local woman with three children. One was strapped to her chest, one was slung over her back, and one was tightly holding her hand. Only the child holding her hand was awake. The other two were blissfully (to me) fast asleep. I pointed to the woman and said to David: "If you don't sleep through the night, I'm going to give you away to that woman."

To this day, I'm not sure what convinced him. After all David was only an infant when I made my threat. But from that day on, he slept through the night. Now he's eighteen and I can hardly get him up.

How to get a child to go to sleep and stay asleep is the subject I *still* get the most phone calls about. In my practice, when I'm talking with parents about their concerns, at least 70 percent of that time is devoted to sleep problems. It's also the area I sympathize with the most. Lack of sleep is what makes parenting so difficult. There is no escaping the exhaustion. There is no time off, no opportunity to catch up on lost sleep.

Chances are good that whatever those parents have tried, I've been there and done that. This book is my gift to all those parents.

The book is divided by ages, or really by stages, corresponding to the natural developmental sleep stages. They are 0–3 months, newborns; 3–12 months, babyhood; 12–36 months, toddlers; and 3–6 years old, preschoolers. You'll notice that within each age category the tips are in random order—you don't start at #1 and then try #2. Rather, I hope you read them all so you see the wide variety of options you have. The emphasis is on safety and well-being. So there's a lot of information on Sudden Infant Death Syndrome (SIDS) and how to help prevent it. Over the years, conventional wisdom has changed: Formerly, it was advocated that babies be placed on their belly to sleep, and now the position of choice is on the back. You will also see why sheepskin should stay on the sheep; it's no longer considered healthy for infants.

I offer a lot of tips on how to treat illnesses that cause sleep to be interrupted and how to distinguish illness from a child's reluctance or refusal to sleep. Illness definitely seems worse in the night—the dark seems to strangely illuminate the symptoms. I include many tips for ways to relieve the tiny patient and the worried parent. But many tips are rooted in today's soil—included are "special circumstances" like divorce, adoption, and twins, all as they relate to sleep.

Within each group you'll find humor tucked between the practical suggestions. Sometimes I've included a tip that was given to me by just one parent in my practice or a parent who wrote in to my Web site: *www.drpaula.com*. (These tips are called "parent-to-parent.") If it works for one child, it might work for another, and again, I include it as long as it is safe.

I may even seem to contradict myself from time to time. So on one page I say "don't let the child sleep in your bed," and then later the advice is "let the child sleep with you." One tip tells you never to give your child alcohol, and that's followed later by the story of the waiter who slipped a little wine into my son David's bottle. I even give you the pros and cons of the very same issue. (See my tips on using or not using an intercom.) But my first priority is: Do no harm. It would be impossible to do a book about sleep without addressing the question of perception (see tip #70). Just recently there was a new-mothers' group in my office. Two mothers were in stark contrast to each other. One who was tearfully blinking and blotting her eyes said her baby was not sleeping at all, and it was just unacceptable. Another mother, the picture of calm, said things were going pretty well with her infant. When they were asked to outline how much each baby was sleeping, it turned out that both babies were sleeping the *exact* same number of hours. It is often the parents who are having the sleeping problem. This really is a case of whether you choose to see the baby bottle as half full or half empty.

I've always wondered why the phrase "to sleep like a baby" seems to mean long, peaceful hours. That's just a beautiful fantasy. I understand only too well that it can get very dark at night, both literally and metaphorically. The other day, a very kind, loving mother confessed to me that in the middle of the night she had slapped her four-year-old daughter who just would not go to sleep. The mother said, "I don't know what came over me." Two days later, sitting in my office, she said she could still feel the sting in her hand. Obviously it was an emotional sting. This book is meant to be an antidote to that kind of desperation.

Understand that sleep is really the ultimate separation for a baby. He is giving up all the good things he has accumulated—smiles, kisses, milk. It's not so easy to exit this fun world. Letting go is unnatural and needs to be learned—here are 365 ways to teach them to your child.

0-3 Months: Newborns

Do not take your baby's sleep habits personally

The first rule is: Do not take it personally when your baby has trouble sleeping.

Babies don't have sleep problems—their parents do. There is no good reason for infants to sleep straight through the night except to have happier parents in the morning. In the pursuit of this happiness, tired parents, particularly moms, have been known to try just about anything. Some of my parents don't always tell me all the things they have tried in their quest to get a baby to go to sleep. I've known parents to sneak off to get advice from just about anyone. In the end, as long as the baby is safe, whatever it takes is okay. (Just share the tip with me so I can pass it along!)

0-3 MONTHS: NEWBORNS

Don't fill up baby on cereal

Don't bother giving your baby cereal in his bottle at night. That's just a popular myth. Lots of people believe that filling up a baby's belly at night with cereal in a bottle will help the baby stay asleep longer. The flawed reasoning is that the cereal acts like cement in his stomach, which will keep him down. Actually, cereal at a very young age can cause indigestion and lead to more sleep problems. Besides, cereal should *not* be started before six months of age, and then it should be offered on a spoon, not in a bottle. Cereal clogs up the nipple hole, making it harder to suck and causing increased swallowing of air. It also invites bacterial contamination of the formula.

It's also been my experience that if you eat a big meal late at night, you are less likely to drift off to dream land and more likely to have nightmares—if you fall asleep at all.

Myth: If a breastfeeding mother drinks wine, she will lull the baby to sleep

Another myth that has been around a *long* time is that a breastfeeding mother who drinks wine or any alcoholic beverage will lull the baby into lengthier sleep. According to a recent study, infants exposed to even small amounts of alcohol in their mother's breastmilk show *altered* sleep patterns, sleeping less and for a shorter time.

So breastfeeding mothers should watch their alcohol intake—they are drinking for two. Also, drinking can make mom a little less sharp. I recall the mom who called frantically because she saw a red spatter on her infant's diaper. On closer inspection she sheepishly confessed it looked a lot like the red cabernet she drank in hopes of getting her baby to sleep. Alcohol, when given directly or indirectly to infants, can lead to irreversible brain and liver injury. So skip the Guinness Stout many nannies recommend, and stick to water or juice.

TIP

0-3 MONTHS: NEWBORNS

Breastfed babies versus bottle-fed babies

It's a fact of life that breastfed babies do wake up in the first six months of life more frequently than bottle-fed babies. They wake more often because they simply cannot down as much milk as a bottle-fed baby. Breastfed babies work very hard to get the milk and tire out early. This is why mothers who pump their breastmilk see that babies need larger quantities of milk then they are able to pump. So just be prepared to be up more often.

Put baby on his back

When it's time for sleep, babies should be put on their backs. The American Academy of Pediatrics, citing research on SIDS prevention, recently released statements that say that babies should not be placed on their bellies to sleep.

The position of choice today is on the back. It makes it harder for some babies to sleep. And parents feel very guilty if a baby sometimes sleeps on her belly. There are ways you can help baby be more comfortable on her back, and there are precautions to take when baby resists and insists on rolling onto her belly to sleep.

Swaddling

If your baby is jittery and has trouble sleeping, particularly because he is on his back, try swaddling him. Sometimes being wrapped up snugly will encourage relaxation and sleep. Most babies like being swaddled because it is more like being back in the womb. Here's how to swaddle a baby: Turn one corner of a blanket down, off center; put the baby on the blanket a little to one side; wrap the shorter end around his body, and then fold the bottom corner up; now take the long end and wrap it all the way around him. The arms should be in the blanket for the first weeks and out of the blanket by the second month.

Ventilate the crib

In order for a baby to sleep safely on her back, there are other requirements. The crib should be well ventilated. Air needs to circulate through the slats. Once in the crib, avoid the use of bumpers, which can restrict the flow of air. If you choose to cover your baby with a blanket, be sure it is tightly tucked and baby is positioned near to the foot of the crib so he can't creep further down under the blanket.

A strongly suspected culprit in SIDS is the accumulation of rebreathed air that can occur when a baby sleeps facedown. Carbon dioxide, the waste product of breathing, can slow the brain's alert mechanism by accumulating around an infant's face. Poorly ventilated rooms, cramped sleeping areas, loose bedding, and even stuffed animals too close to the child's face can all contribute to an increase in carbon dioxide, which in turn may result in cessation of breathing—and SIDS.

Sleep whenever the baby sleeps

This is really rule #1, but we just got to it: The golden rule for new parents is: You sleep whenever the baby is asleep. I had a wonderful supervisor when I was a resident, who likened the internship to the first months of a newborn's life. She said her job was to raise me from residency to doctorhood. She said, "When you see food, eat it; when you pass a bathroom, use it; and when you spy a bed, lie in it." Mothers need to follow similar advice. When your baby sleeps, you should sleep as well. Don't decide this is the time to write thank-yous or straighten up the house. Don't think you need to get things done. You may really need to keep them "undone." At least for a little while.

Don't let the baby fall asleep on you

The previous rule, however, doesn't mean that when you sleep, the sleeping baby should always be attached to you. For the first few weeks, there is nothing more reassuring to the baby than physical contact, but after that, it is time to think of separating yourself from her just as she is about to fall into a deep sleep. I've heard mothers in my new-mothers' groups complain, "Now what do I do? I've finally got the baby to sleep and I can't move." When I ask why, they answer, "Because I'm UNDER the baby."

Don't let baby sleep with a bottle

Warning: Do not leave a bottle in your baby's mouth after he falls asleep. You don't want him to become accustomed to drinking while sleeping; he will look for a bottle each time he wakens. It's also dangerous, since he can choke on the fluid. The constant pressure of the bottle can cause dental misalignment, and the sugar in juice or milk can cause tooth decay and destruction and even affect the permanent teeth. If you need another reason, the milk or juice can spill onto his skin and cause nasty rashes.

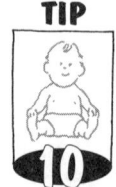

No bottle, continued: Feed baby <u>before</u> bed

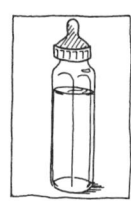

Going to bed with a bottle is an invitation to obesity. Some babies can drink as much as 30 ounces of formula through the night in an effort to get to sleep. The result is an overfed baby. If your baby is hungry, he should be fed before he's put down for sleep time.

TIP 11

Not all cribs are created equal

Often, parents will purchase extra cribs for traveling or to leave at a family member's house. Unfortunately, items such as portacribs and hand-carry pop-up cribs are not necessarily safe. Don't be lulled by the word *crib* on the package. Some portacribs, for example, can easily collapse, and some have soft bottoms—they are designed that way so they can fold up easily, but they aren't recommended for an infant who sleeps facedown. The incidence of SIDS isn't confined to happening in full-sized cribs; it can happen in any unsafe sleep environment. Make sure any device you use as a substitute crib meets all safety criteria—firm mattress, etcetera.

Overlying

There are lots of myths that creep in at night along with the baby. Have you heard the one about the parent who rolled over during the night and crushed the baby? There is actually an official name for this—it's called overlying. There are some instances when you shouldn't have a baby next to you: If a parent is obese or temporarily under the influence of any medication or substance that could deepen their level of sleep, then it should be avoided. But true overlying is less frequent than rumor would have it. One way to guard against overlying is to buy a "side sleeper" or resting device that is a separate bed within your bed.

It's been my observation over the years that most mothers respond to just about every move their newborn makes. You know your own sleep behavior: If you have always slept through fire alarms, maybe cosleeping is not for you.

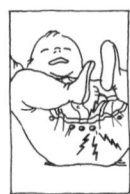

Correct sleep attire (newborns)

Babies *should never* wear infant "kimonos," because they can get tangled in them. Even worse, most of them come with a drawstring at the bottom, which could definitely get tangled around a baby. Don't buy them! Make sure baby is in a garment meant for sleep—that includes being flame retardant. (Interestingly, only nightclothes are mandated to be flame retardant.) Avoid sleepwear with snaps, zippers, or buttons—they can come off and be swallowed, and zippers can catch the baby's skin.

Don't buy footed blanket sleepers, unless they are completely cotton right down to the tippy-toe. I have treated many children with itchy feet caused by sweat buildup in the plastic lined soles of their footed pj's. Choose breathable fabrics even for the footcover.

TIP

I'm often asked if baby should be dressed on the "cold" or the "warm" side. I say err on the cool side. Heat can increase an infant's temperature and mimic a fever, and possibly cause rashes.

Myth: "Did you hear the one about the cat..."

Someone (maybe a dog lover) started the one about a cat jumping on a sleeping baby's face to lick off any leftover milk. Although widely repeated, this has never, ever been documented. So it's not necessary to send your beloved cat away when you bring baby home from the hospital. On the other hand, cats can be quite jealous and have been known to hiss at the newcomer. Generally, they just retreat to some hidden corner to mope over being replaced.

Mosquito netting

To make sure your baby is safe from any stray animals, including very tiny ones with wings, you might consider buying one of those wonderful new mosquito nettings that zip over the top of the crib. In this day and age when mosquitoes can be downright dangerous, if you live in a temperate or warm climate and keep windows open, keep baby zipped up at night. Netting keeps out all such pesky pests.

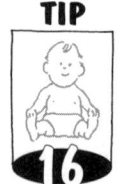

Cranial molding (AKA flat head)

Now that babies are sleeping on their backs, there is a problem called cranial molding—technically referred to as plagiocephaly. (Also often referred to, less technically, as a "flat head.") A little anatomy lesson is in order: Babies are born with flexible skulls with many overlapping flat bones. That's a good thing. The flexibility of the skull allows babies to emerge through the birth canal without too much damage to the mom. It also accommodates their growing brains by sliding apart as the brain grows. Unfortunately it also means that babies' heads are easily shaped, or misshaped, by whatever position or location a baby has slept in. (Understand that not all cultures desire round heads. For example, the Blackfoot tribe used to put babies in pointy-headed cradles in order to mold their heads to a point. *We* happen to like round heads.) Today, with baby sleeping on his back, there is a "problem"—not a medical one—of baby developing a flattened head.

Flat head, continued

Some babies are born with a seriously molded head due to the trauma of the birth experience or because of compression in a tight or misshapen uterus. I tell parents in *these* cases not to have baby sleep flat but to let the baby sleep at a very slight elevation. Just put a rolled-up towel under the head of the mattress. This takes advantage of some of the abdominal muscles that babies have even as young as one month. She can pull up ever so slightly and essentially ease the pressure of the weight of her head off the bed.

Just say no...to soft surfaces

There is a concern that you might place baby on a soft surface and his face could sink in, obstructing breathing. Everyone thinks of "soft and cuddly" when they think of newborns, and also "warm and mushy." The fact is we now know that a likely cause of crib death is due to babies' rebreathing their own air. This can happen when the baby's face is toward a soft surface. Here's what we know: There is a center in the brain that recognizes the level of carbon dioxide and oxygen. In infants, this mechanism isn't fine-tuned, and in some babies it is actually defective. So when the carbon dioxide rises, instead of triggering the baby to move her face and breathe more rapidly to get rid of the carbon dioxide, the mechanism shuts down. Unfortunately the results can be deadly.

Just say no...to sheepskin

Do not put your baby to sleep on a lamb or sheepskin fleece. The idea of cradling your baby in a warm and cozy sheepskin may seem appealing, but it can be dangerous. There are two reasons: Many babies can roll over and their faces are directly on the fleece, causing them to be in the rebreathing position in a "trapping" fabric. (The landmark studies of SIDS in New Zealand initially blamed lambskin bedding.) Also the lanolin found in sheepskin can be an allergen that can cause nasal congestion and airway swelling. If you have a lambskin—which was once considered terrific for newborns—throw it on the floor and use it as a rug.

0-3 MONTHS: NEWBORNS

Close to you

The first few weeks of your baby's life, it's probably safest and most convenient to have him sleeping very close to you. The baby wakes often and it's easier to fetch him from beside you than from the next room. You may ask: Why is it okay for the baby to sleep facedown on you on occasion but not facedown in a crib? Good question! Research indicates that a baby who's sleeping on you is actually *moving* a great deal. Your steady breathing is taking the baby up and down. So it's safe to be on her belly when she is on you.

The first six weeks

It makes the most sense to put your newborn in a bassinet, or cradle, or even a carriage next to your bed when you get home from the hospital. This is good for the first six weeks. You have gone through a great body-altering experience and are not ready to run laps or even just walk back and forth to the nursery. It's good for the baby as well. He can be near enough to see you, smell you, hear you. Remember that he spent nine months "indoors" and is not ready to separate just yet. Some sleep experts believe that sleep problems are actually generated by the modern view that encourages early separation for sleep. They suggest the family bed as a solution. For some families it certainly does work out best that way.

The safe bassinet

The bassinet should be small enough so that the baby feels securely surrounded, yet large enough so that when he stretches his arms, they are not hitting the sides. The typical bassinet is 18 inches across and 30 inches in length—and baby is approximately 20 inches long or 25 inches with his arms stretched up above his head. Again, by six weeks most babies outgrow their bassinets and need a larger space to stretch out in, and one that allows air to circulate through the slats. Any baby able to roll over is definitely too old to be in a bassinet regardless of their weight.

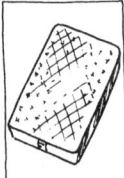

The mattress

Finding the right place for a baby to sleep may sound a little bit like playing "Goldilocks": This one may be too hard, that one too soft, and finally you'll find the one that is just right. The mattress doesn't have to be hard and stiff—just firm enough so baby can't sink into it. Make sure the mattress isn't made of animal hair, as in the past, because some babies will have an allergic reaction to it. The crib and mattress are best bought as a unit, as a snug fit is vital for safety reasons. You should not be able to slip your hand between the mattress and the slats of the crib.

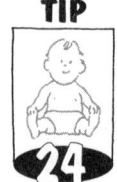

Sheets

Make sure the sheets are fitted. Sometimes sheets are borrowed from another child and could be stretched out. The sheets shouldn't clump up, so baby can move or jiggle. Put a 100 percent cotton sheet on the mattress because babies are unlikely to be allergic to it. Also, cotton just breathes better—carbon dioxide can pass through the cotton faster than it does through polyester. Sometimes it won't pass through polyester at all.

You don't want anything that can obstruct a child's breathing. This also means you want whatever is under the mattress to be 100 percent cotton as well.

Another recent improvement is a crib sheet that has extra wide ticking across the under-width, so it cannot be pulled off the mattress. Typically sheets can be pulled off with just 31 pounds of pull, whereas these new safer sheets require a 121-pound pull to dislodge it. They also come with allergy barriers, but it's not clear how the barrier affects carbon dioxide retention. Be on the lookout for new studies.

TIP

Just say no...to pillows

Babies don't need pillows, even though pillows are sold to you in newborn blanket sets. If she sleeps on a pillow, she may bend her neck in a way that could make it harder for her to breathe freely. Also, the softness of the pillow might allow the baby's head to sink into it and create a pocket in which the baby might suffocate. You can, however, have baby bumpers if they are narrow and tightly secured to the sides of the crib. (The only time you might want a pillow is if baby has a cold—more about that later—and then you want to slightly elevate baby. But even then the pillow goes under the mattress, not under baby's head.) Avoid down bedding of any kind; it's bad for allergies and for safety reasons as well.

Be careful of makeshift sleeping areas

There can be a problem with homemade and makeshift sleeping areas. For example, some parents create a sleeping area by placing a pillow inside an enclosed playpen. Playpens are called *play*pens for a reason; they are not designed for sleep. So don't use one as a crib unless you happen to have one of the newer playpens that come with a hard bottom meant for sleep. The problem is the same one of baby being able to retain carbon monoxide. When in doubt, an open blanket on the floor would be a safe choice if a crib were not available.

Go on night patrol for safety

Every night you should check the crib for anything that could have fallen into it—the cap off the diaper cream tube, your toddler's Barbie doll shoe, and so forth. Babies tend to grasp whatever is there and pull it right into their mouth. One of the many nice things about having a baby is that they get a lot of presents—stuffed animals, rattles, mobiles. But nothing should be left in the crib that can be chewed or bitten off. I still remember the baby who swallowed a teddy bear's blue eye. The good news was that he didn't choke on it. You would be amazed by the grip of baby's jaw. (Maybe you forgot what it felt like when you breastfed. Ouch!)

The surface your baby sleeps on should be free of all snaps, buttons, and zippers. This rule is also aimed at YOU sleeping more peacefully, knowing you have made your baby's environment safe while he sleeps.

Let baby fall asleep in his crib

If you help your baby fall asleep in his bassinet or crib, he will be able to do it on his own much sooner. (And you will avoid sleep problems later on.) Your baby can eventually learn to put himself to sleep, but you can't expect him to go cold turkey from rocking on your nice warm body to just being put down in a crib still awake. When the baby is starting to fall asleep—his eyelids are fluttering—carry him to his crib before he is asleep and put him down gently while still leaving your hand on him. You continue to do this until he gets used to the idea of falling asleep on his own.

The last thing that a baby remembers

When you put your baby down in her crib, the last thing she remembers before falling asleep will be the first thing she searches for during the night when her normal sleep pattern lightens and she wakes. If the last thing was your warm arms or a bottle in her mouth, and she can't replace it, she will invariably cry. What you *would* like her to be remembering is the nice comfortable mattress. It's always there for her.

Transferring baby

Parents often tell me that they rock baby to sleep in their bed or in their arms and then very, very carefully transfer the baby to his crib. Lo and behold, in 15 minutes, if not sooner, baby is up and wailing. (Review tip #30, "The last thing that a baby remembers.") Look at it this way: How would you react if you went to sleep in a Hilton and woke up in a Motel 6? I'd complain!

I still vividly recall trying to lower my daughter into the crib while she continued to nurse. Dangling my breast over the crib rail did nothing for my getting any sleep. And of course when she woke up she immediately looked around for that same dangling breast! (It took me a while to learn all the rules, too.)

Babies like to suck...pacifiers

Some babies suck their fingers while still in utero—we know that from sonograms. These babies need to suck, so give them a pacifier from the get-go. If you use a pacifier to put your child to sleep, remember to remove it once she has nodded off. It would be best if the need was limited to falling asleep, not staying asleep.

Hostage to the pacifier?

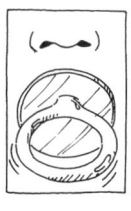

If your baby goes to sleep with a pacifier in her mouth and then wakes and can't find it, she will cry. So make sure there are several in the crib she can easily reach. However, *never* tie a pacifier to the crib. Even if it is a short string, there is always the danger of strangling. I don't like *any* device that clips or attaches the pacifier to the baby. Somehow they manage to roam and get clipped where they are not wanted—like onto baby's skin.

I have seen overwhelming proof that babies are clever and calculating as early as three months. One of my moms swore that her infant could count. She demonstrated by videotaping how she left four pacifiers each night in her four-month-old's crib. Her baby would push the first three pacifiers out of the crib one by one while attempting to rally a parent with her wailing. She would stop just before pushing out the *last* pacifier. Once she figured out no one was coming in, she would plant the fourth one firmly into her mouth.

TIP

"Stimulate" your baby to sleep

There are several ways to stimulate your baby to go to sleep—yes, that seems like a paradox, but it isn't really. One way is through a mobile. Mobiles can be so hypnotic that they put adults to sleep. Some come with music, some without. My personal favorites are the black and white ones like the ones with cows that have the cows facing the baby. These mobiles also have changeable pieces to match the visual development of your growing infant. Be sure the mobile is placed high enough so that baby can't reach it.

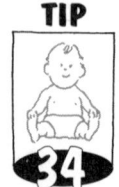

Music soothes—Sing

Music is almost always soothing. Babies respond to the sound of your voice. It doesn't matter what you sing as long as it's repetitive and boring, which is the whole point. Babies don't get bored the way we do, so pick songs you can repeat over and over. The whole idea is to make your baby sleepy. If the words keep changing, the baby may stay up just to listen. (My own mother used to croon "Aye Aye Ba-by, Aye Aye Ba-by" over and over, and I am a very good sleeper to this very day.)

Be a one-parent band

You can actually be a musician, even if you can't play a note and are tone deaf. Remember the popular off-Broadway musical *STOMP*—that's the one where the performers banged on garbage cans with kitchen utensils. All that matters is that you establish a beat. If you need assistance, you can purchase the Music Maker—a zither-like instrument that comes with song sheets that show you exactly which notes to play. This has been around a long time. Just keep the beat droning and monotonous.

Stuffed animals with a beat

Try one of the specially designed stuffed animals, often in the shape of a bear, that simulate uterine sounds. These aren't to play with, just to listen to. I have a mother in my practice who had her fetal heartbeat recorded by her husband while she was in labor in the delivery room. She swears this "virtual" beat worked. This often works only for a brief period of time—usually until the baby sort of "hatches" at about three months. Chances are good you will receive one, or more, as a gift. (Don't return any of them.)

Transitional objects, part I

Try holding a cloth diaper while you are nursing or feeding, and then put that cloth diaper in the crib *along* with baby. The smell the cloth acquires from your body, plus just the association of it being there in your arms, is sometimes enough to make baby sleep. This is an early example of a transitional object, which is just what it sounds like. This helps the baby make the transition from one place to another, from your arms to the crib, from being awake to being asleep. Just don't wash the object too often, and keep it simple. It's hard to replace any special, one-of-a-kind item. Go for the plain white diaper.

Napping

During the newborn period, there is almost no such thing as "napping"— all the little bits of time your baby is in shut-eye mode add up to the total amount of sleep the baby is getting each day. After the first six weeks, many babies have somewhat longer stretches of sleep. Napping doesn't interfere with the development of lengthier nighttime periods of sleep until about six months. Napping is part of the *total* sleep time your infant needs as well as being one of her main activities. Napping also doesn't have to occur in the traditional sleeping-at-night location; it can occur almost anywhere. You may even be lucky enough to have a baby who naps when you go out for a walk.

Catnaps: On <u>your</u> belly

If your baby doesn't sleep easily during the day, put him down for little catnaps. A good place, which is always available, is on your belly. If you worry about the baby falling off, try lying on the floor. This is good for your back as well. Pull your knees up and lay the baby out on your chest and abdomen like a bear rug. If someone can sneak in quietly and capture just the two of you, this makes for a great photo opportunity.

Catnaps: Try a Snugli

Baby can catnap or even sleep in a Snugli—that way at least your hands are free, and your baby will love the motion. Get one with a neck extension piece so baby's head can rest comfortably. If you have a bad or weak back—or your baby weighs more than 10 pounds—try Sara's Ride, a side sling that distributes the weight better.

Catnaps: Swing time

You can try a swing, as long as you are in attendance at all times. Don't worry about the length of time baby spends swinging. Get a swing that can be put in a reclining as well as a sitting position. While it's in the reclining position, layer the seat with a soft blanket and secure the lap belt. Just don't put the baby in the all-the-way back position. You can't really see her and the air circulation could be poor. Buy a battery-operated version, not the windup type. (The minute it winds down, it makes an awful loud ratchet sound that inevitably wakes baby up.)

You can often pick a swing up at a garage sale, but check it carefully for balance.

Keep a sleep diary

Track your baby's sleep patterns with a chart, particularly if you are concerned about the length of time your baby sleeps or doesn't seem to sleep. A new mom will often tell me that her baby never sleeps. A record of the amount of time baby sleeps often provides perspective. If you add up all the time sleeping (and remember, napping counts, too), you'll see the baby is probably sleeping more than you think.

It's very important that you understand that babies sleep the amount of time they need to.

Cozy napping place

You can create a warm, cozy napping place by using a hot water bottle that is well wrapped in insulated material such as terry cloth. Fill it three-quarters full with lukewarm water. Put the baby on his side and gently tuck the water bottle along his belly. It gives a nice sensation of warmth and motion and can also be helpful in other situations of high stress or discomfort as he grows.

There are wonderful hot water bottle covers that come in comfy fabrics and sweet animal shapes, which add to the experience.

The Nikken

There is a new device out made by the Japanese called Nikken. It is based on the Asian theory that we all emit electromagnetic waves. One of the reasons babies don't sleep so well, according to the creators of Nikken, is that baby's electromagnetic waves are interfered with by all the waves we are exposed to, from microwaves, electric power lines, radios and TVs, and so forth. The device is harmless. You put the magnet under the sheet and, according to the marketing material, baby will sleep better. (For more information call 1-800-669-8859.)

Just say no...to a newborn crying in her crib

It's very important to remember that at this age, the baby should not be left in her crib to cry. If she cries, she is in some distress. If she can't fall asleep after about five minutes, then she belongs back in your arms. The newborn should have only pleasant associations with her crib. Don't ever use the crib as a "jail" or put her in it with an angry or punishing gesture. The crib will be your friend for at least the first two years of your child's life; don't transform it into your enemy.

To make the crib even more friendly, put a smiling picture of yourself on the inside of the crib, and a Mylar-type mirror.

The two-hour rule

A good rule of thumb is to put your newborn down to sleep about once every two hours. Longer sleep sets in by two months or when baby is 13 pounds. There's nothing magical or mystical about 13 pounds, it's just that many babies weigh in at around 6½ to 7 pounds at birth, and they seem to sleep longer periods when they double their birth weight. As weight increases, so does organ size. At this weight, babies can now take in larger quantities of milk at a time and not get indigestion, whereas newborns need to be refueled more often.

FYI: How much sleep does a baby need?

1–3 months	15–15.5 hours
6 months	14 hours
12 months	13–14 hours
2 years	13 hours
5 years	11 hours

Never wake a sleeping baby unless...

Newborns are expected to lose as much as 10 percent of their birth weight during the first week. Once they figure out how to suck efficiently, they begin to put back that weight and then some. Never wake a sleeping baby unless you have the rare newborn who sleeps so much that he doesn't regain the necessary ounces by the two-week checkup. These babies need to be woken up every two to three hours to feed until the weight is regained.

Parents may think that a newborn who always sleeps is a blessing, but babies who are rarely awake may not be thriving. It's critical that babies take in enough nourishment to make urine and stool. To do that, they can't sleep through *all* their meals. If your pediatrician directs you to feed your infant more often, gently waken your baby by fully undressing her to allow a cool breeze or your breath to "tickle" her skin. Or, move your sleeping infant to another room and let more light in to help her wake enough to suck. Never shake a baby!

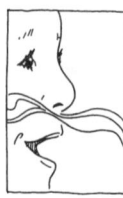

Aromatherapy

Parents have told me of preparing different aromatic mixtures that help babies stay asleep. Mix a small amount of chamomile with some lavender and make a sachet using a porous cotton cloth. You can place the pouch under the sheet at the head of the baby's crib. This is really a variation of aromatherapy. There are alternative health providers who attribute a variety of near miraculous healing qualities to various scents. It doesn't seem to hurt—scents such as chamomile or sandalwood are known to be calming.

Caution: Be careful not to use too pungent an aroma or you might end up stimulating your infant instead of calming him. Some scents, such as eucalyptus and wintergreen, can be too powerful for infants. It can even cause an oil-derived burn in the airways if the concentration is too high, or bleeding if taken internally. So, to be safe, use these scents in their cool versions only; do not heat up, and be certain baby cannot get it into his mouth.

Use a wedge system

Studies indicate that snugly surrounding your infant makes for longer sleep periods. There are systems designed to keep baby on her back while sleeping. These are basically cloth-covered foam shapes that prevent baby from turning over. That's a good thing, because babies who roll over are subject to the risk of lying facedown and collecting carbon dioxide. Any wedge system you purchase should be FDA approved and its intended use should be for SIDS prevention. The wedge should be secured to the crib in a way that won't permit baby to put her face down into it.

Use a halo to snuggle her head

There are halo-type wedges that turn baby into a little sleeping angel. Adding a wedge that surrounds your infant's head seems to further lengthen sleep time. One wedge, called the Halo System, was designed by parents specifically to prevent a SIDS event. This system includes a mattress with a fan underneath it that sucks away the carbon dioxide, so that even a baby who sleeps on her belly is safe. This is FDA approved. I find it rather nifty. (For more information, call 1-888-999-4256.)

Put a hat on her head

Some studies have indicated that babies with a hat on sleep better through the night. I know it initially sounds strange to put on a hat when the baby is staying in, but my advice is to try anything that might work—as long as it is safe. A hat may just be another way of achieving a swaddling effect.

No ties on the hat please and use cotton. Some hats are too snug and could give your baby a headache or even compromise the blood flow to the scalp.

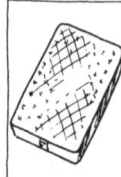

Nature's Cradle

A child-development company run by pediatricians, called Infant Advantage, created a system that has FDA approval for sleep training. It softly hums and gently rocks your baby into slumber and reportedly makes baby smarter (!), too. A gently rocking mattress is accompanied by soft amniotic sounds and the comforting rhythm of a mother's heartbeat. According to research, use of this device results in your baby sleeping through the night 70 percent sooner, causes your baby to cry 65 percent less, and causes your baby to score higher on the three-month Brazelton neonatal assessment test. (For more information, call 1-800-452-9651.)

Jiggle the bassinet

Movement seems to facilitate sleep. Many infant "containers" are built with some sort of a jiggling mechanism and have been for all of recorded history. ("The cradle will rock…") Strollers and carriages usually have spring actions on the wheels. Although your bassinet may not be designed for motion, it still can be jiggled by just gently moving it back and forth and side to side. Do not fear that you could induce "shaken baby syndrome"— you are nowhere near that level of jiggling. Just make sure you are indeed jiggling the bassinet. One night I jiggled so hard the floor lamp fell over.

Go for a car ride

No one knows why, but most babies fall asleep in the car. It is probably the vibrations and the noise, but it works. Make sure your baby is in a safety-approved infant car seat. She should be dressed for sleep, with a clean diaper. (And don't go driving around if she has just eaten!) If you get the speed just right and avoid lights, you can move along without braking. Parents tell me the baby invariably wakes up when they stop for a light. So choose a route that doesn't include stop signs or too many traffic lights.

Attach a mechanical crib jiggler

A pediatrician invented this after he discovered his newborn would sleep only while he was driving at a steady 55 mph. (See tip #56.) The local police knew the good doctor would often drive at night and they wouldn't ticket him when he went through the one stop sign in his way. Call 1-800-NOCOLIC for more information about the sleep tight jiggler that simulates the feel of riding in a car at about 55 mph—without leaving the crib. It also saves on gas!

Drifting lullabies

It's been noted that music soothes the "savage" beast—it works equally well on the "tiny" variety. Soft music, in fact, calms and can help most babies go to sleep. The best kind of music is songs that drift off—whether you sing it or it's on the tape recorder and you gradually turn the volume down. Although I sometimes advocate repetitive music or beats, the tempo and content *do* matter. This is not the time for any song that is interactive, that requires your child to mimic you. "Wheels on the Bus" and "Monkeys on the Bed" are perfectly good songs, but they wind the child up, not down.

Babies like to suck...fingers

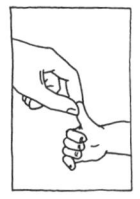

At about six weeks of age, a baby may discover his thumb and that it is part of his body. Unlike a pacifier, his thumb is always available and can't be misplaced. If it becomes "lost," you can put it back in. Do not discourage thumb sucking at this time; in fact, you should encourage him to suck his fingers to comfort himself. Grandma may tell you that thumb sucking is bad for his teeth, but not sleeping is worse. Usually babies just give it up on their own at about five or six months.

Quiet down the environment

Plan in advance, especially with a newborn. You want to prepare the environment so that it is compatible with sleep. Treat your living space as if you have entered a movie theater. You know the rules: *Shut off* all electrical devices—phones, cell phones, beepers, noisy fax machines. (If you have to, put your beeper on vibrator.) Put a piece of tape over the doorbell or hang a sign that says: "Do not buzz." Absolutely nothing is worse than having a sleeping baby jarred awake by a door-to-door aluminum siding salesman.

Wake a sleeping baby for dinner

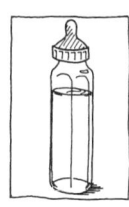

If you have a baby who is a champion afternoon napper, you could end up with a baby who skips a meal and is up all night. So wake him for his evening feed. Joining the rest of the family for dinner is a habit you will want to encourage eventually, and you can start right here.

Hum tunelessly

Let's say you are hoarse from last night's lullabies and too lazy to get up to turn on the radio or wind up his mobile. Don't move. Hold baby against your chest and just hum.

Mmmmmmmmmmmmmmmmmmmmmmmmmmm mmmmmmmmmmmmmmmmmmmm.

Cozy warmed mittens and booties

Throw mittens and booties briefly into the dryer to warm them. This works a lot like the hat—it contains the baby like swaddling. If baby is a thumb sucker, then make sure to cut a hole for the thumb.

Nip sleep problems in the bud

You are doing your baby a huge favor by establishing and sticking to a nighttime routine. The fact is that 25 to 30 percent of *all* children experience some kind of sleep difficulty. And most children don't just outgrow their sleep problems like they do their pj's with the little frog feet. Children with sleep problems may grow up to be adults with insomnia. Just because sleep problems are common doesn't mean they go away. Take positive action from the newborn period on to avoid the likelihood of adult sleep problems.

Teaching day versus night

Babies are not born understanding the difference between day and night. Make sure your newborn is exposed to sunlight during the day and kept in a darkened room at night to help establish the day-night pattern. We all have a pineal gland in our brain—sometimes referred to as the "third eye"—which responds to light and dark by secreting hormones that help us sleep. When the lights are on, fewer of these hormones are secreted.

More on day/night confusion

Usually day/night confusion disappears at around three months when babies become more wakeful during the day and sleep more at night. This coincides with the establishment of hormone cycles. (Sleep is less influenced by hunger than by hormones.) Melatonin, Mother Nature's sleeping pill, is released at night, inducing drowsiness and relaxing muscles. Sleep is also influenced by cortisol levels, which drop off after 4 P.M. and are influenced by melatonin. It's a complicated system that all works in sync if given the opportunity.

The six-week miracle

You can expect at six weeks of age, that babies will sleep longer, with the exception of premature babies (in which case you have to take into consideration what "age" they really are and be lenient in your expectation). Premature babies are not only neurologically immature, but they need to make up for all those calories and hormones they missed from mommy's body via the umbilical cord. Since twins are often premature, parents are often doubly "blessed" with newborns who take longer to sleep through the night. I often quote the line "consistency is the hobgoblin of small minds"—*except* in the case of twins and sleep. Then you must establish rules early on both fronts.

TIP

Understanding colic

No one knows what colic really is except that it usually translates to a sleepless night. The word *colic* is from the Greek "kolikos," relating to the colon, but there's no evidence it has anything to do with the colon or abdominal problems. What we do know is that colic is associated with hours of screaming, or crying, and often occurs at the same time of day. It often begins at two or three weeks of age and usually disappears by three to four months. It is not a specific condition, so there is no antidote. Just remember as miserable as your child may seem, she is not ill. Motion seems to inhibit the crying, and then you have a shot at getting some sleep. So review all the ways to jiggle a baby.

Colic and sleep

Infants who have colic sleep less than infants who do not. They wake more often and require more parental control in order to establish healthy sleep habits. In general, poor sleep habits are learned, but difficulty falling asleep can be inborn. If baby continues to have sleep problems, it is probably due to the parents' inability to establish regular patterns and schedules when the colic disappears. At this age, crying is often fatigue driven. It becomes a vicious cycle—with less sleep everyone is more irritable and needs more sleep.

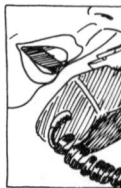

Perception is everything

Don't be concerned about all the people who ask if your newborn baby is sleeping. It is painful for parents to hear about how well other babies are sleeping. And yet, even perfect strangers seem compelled to comment on it in the park. In my mother's group there was one mother crying about how little her baby sleeps. The other mother was smiling and happy about how much her baby sleeps. When we compared notes, it turned out that both babies were sleeping the *exact* same number of hours. You may count waking differently from your neighbor. Most mothers become so sensitive to the baby that when baby stirs, they wake up and nurse at the first sound of fussing. Some mothers don't count this as waking up. Others feel beleaguered by every nighttime round of feeding.

Count "feeding" as sleeping time!

One mom shared the fact that her baby sleeps through the night. Actually, it turned out he gets up every two hours to feed, but because he sleeps through the feeding, the mother counts it as sleeping. She was quite mellow about it. Again, this has to do with seeing the cradle half-full as opposed to half-empty, so-to-speak. If you count the number of hours baby sleeps as including time spent feeding, this leads to your thinking your baby sleeps for longer periods, and you may not feel as tired or frustrated.

Don't let an infant cry herself to sleep

I don't believe in letting a newborn baby or an infant cry herself to sleep. Period. Sometimes a baby will continue to cry after you have put her down. Wait five to ten minutes—the time it should take for your baby to fall asleep. It is also about as long as your newborn can keep her image of you in her head without really panicking. This is also about as long as most parents can reasonably be expected to tolerate the noise. If the crying doesn't stop, then you need to return to the room at about five-minute intervals.

Keep baby's arm down

We do know that the incidence of SIDS is higher in babies who sleep on their tummy. Further, there are more SIDS events in babies who sleep on their belly with their arms up along the side of their face. This is because the baby's arm traps the carbon dioxide between the airway and the arm. In the first three months, if your baby insists on sleeping on her belly, make sure her arm is down, even if you have to swaddle it down.

Positional molding

Have your baby sleep on alternating sides as well as on his back. If you are really concerned about your baby developing a flat head, simply move the baby's head position, alternating direction from night to night. Keep in mind the flattening is not medically hazardous and usually will round out spontaneously after baby learns to sit up. Sometimes, however, the flattening just looks so wrong that it is upsetting to parents.

Just say yes...to intercoms

Having a baby monitor is better then having the baby sleep with you, and you waking and responding to her every sound and movement. Parents reach out and touch too often. With an intercom, you can monitor her and know when she is fully awake and needs you. You can control the volume (of the intercom, not the baby) so that you don't hear every sound. This is also a safety measure in a big house where you really can't hear from room to room.

Just say no...to intercoms

Most parents turn the monitor up too high and run in to check the baby at every sound. The slightest gurgle can sound like trucks are rolling through the nursery. Once on vacation with another family, we had all our children sleeping on the back porch with a monitor. We suddenly heard rip-roaring yelling, followed by the sounds of adults. As we ran to the back, we discovered our children were still fast asleep. We realized we were listening in to our next door neighbors—on *our* monitor.

Also, the monitor may give a false sense of security, and parents won't check up enough on a sleeping infant. Obviously, if your child has a medical condition like asthma, you should be checking in face to face.

Be a little flexible (but let the mattress be firm)

Be open to trying alternate sleeping arrangements. That doesn't mean switch locations every night. Just understand that there are nights, and then there are NIGHTS. Don't be afraid to use other sleep locations as long as the mattress is firm and the designated sleep area is safe. Some babies sleep best in their own rooms, others in their parents' room or even in their parents' bed on rare occasions. Choose what's right for your lifestyle. Don't be locked in to preconceived notions of how your baby should be sleeping and where.

Repeat: Infant should not be placed to sleep in a playpen that is not designed for sleep. The mattress may be too soft and unanchored, and baby could even slip underneath it.

Laying on of hands

Laying on of hands can help calm and soothe a baby to sleep. Because he usually has bigger hands, a father can lay one hand on baby's back and the other on baby's head. Patting baby at about 60 beats per minute helps induce sleep. (This is the heartbeat rhythm that baby has grown accustomed to in utero.) Remove hands gradually, one at a time.

Crying baby: Check diaper if baby won't sleep

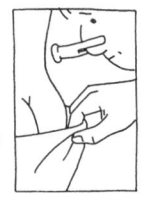

If baby has a big stool in his diaper, it may cause irritation, pain, and crying. If the skin is inflamed by the urine in the stool-loaded diaper, it will certainly keep the baby up. Usually babies don't poop in the middle of the night. But if baby is suddenly crying, take a peek at his diaper (or a whiff will give it away) and change him very quickly, and quietly.

The miracle reflex

Stroke your baby's forehead lightly, right down the middle to the bridge of her nose. This stimulates a reflex that causes her to close her eyes, and she will immediately take a slow, deep breath. Often she will fall asleep. This works until about two months of age. This has been referred to as the miracle reflex.

0-3 MONTHS: NEWBORNS

Expect to rise to the occasion

A good friend came into my hospital room when I had my son David. She handed me a new lipstick and a card. The card read: "I know you will be able to rise to this occasion…about eight times a night." I was already much too tired to appreciate the humor, but that's just the point. Sleepless nights and infants are just a fact of most new parents' lives. There is no way to avoid getting up with a newborn, so expect it and try to maintain your sense of humor. That will definitely come in handy when your newborn turns into a toddler who can talk back. (Note: The lipstick dried up years ago, but I still have the card.)

3-12 Months: Infants

Put the car seat into the crib

Don't wake a baby who is fast asleep in the car. Remove the car seat from the car and put it directly into the crib.

Caveat: The baby will be in a semi-reclining position, which is good for a baby with a cold or who is teething and drooling a lot. However, this is not recommended for newborns because of their poor neck control (they have soft cartilage in their windpipes and flexing the neck can pinch their airway closed). Combined with the angle of the car seat, this could result in a dangerous accumulation of carbon dioxide in the airway.

Play dead

Make the whole family retire early or appear to so child sees that nighttime is for sleeping. It shouldn't be too difficult to convince everyone you are all ready for bed. Remember, children learn from what they see, and many behaviors are learned by imitation and modeling. My children learned very early on to "put Mommy to sleep" some nights, instead of the other way around. They appreciated the special privilege, and I loved the luxury.

Safe sleep position

At this age baby, should still be put to sleep on her back—if she is willing. Babies learn to roll over at about three months and may prefer the belly-down position. If possible, continue to use a wedge, and she may be happy to remain safely supine. If you suddenly take the wedge away, you may be inviting sleep problems. On the other hand, it is difficult to *start* baby on a wedge after the newborn period. Of course, make sure the mattress is firm and the bedding is tightly fitted. It's also critical that you have a pollution- and smoke-free environment.

Naptime: Cradle

One of the ways to help your baby nap is to put her in a cradle. I've always liked cradles, and you already have a cradle if you think about it: You have your arms, a truly wonderful place. There is no reason in the first few months, especially during the day, why you can't sit with the baby napping on you.

Naptime: Infant rocking seat

The baby can even rock *herself* into a nap in an infant rocking seat. The slightest motion by the baby causes more motion. There are many infant bouncing seats with spring action built in. When it gets to gently rocking, it often induces sleep. Don't worry, the baby can't catapult out as long as you remember to always fasten the seatbelt. But avoid the ones that squeak or make noise!

Naptime: Stroller, outdoors

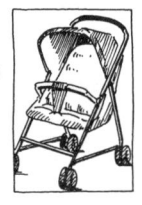

Take the stroller outside. Riding in the stroller can put a baby to sleep—the fresh air and interesting sights add other needed stimulation. It also helps if you find streets that are poorly paved! The bumps are a plus for getting baby to sleep. This gives you a break, and you might meet someone with even more good sleep ideas.

Naptime: Stroller, indoors

When it's too cold outdoors, stroll inside the house. Just put the baby down for a nap in her stroller and push it back and forth over a doorsill. Some strollers, and most larger carriages, have their own spring action built right in.

Jogging with sleeping baby

You can even jog with baby by using one of the new jogging strollers, which come in different age-appropriate sizes. The baby gets safely strapped in and off you both go. Just like taking baby for a car ride, you need to maintain a good pace. Jogging is environmentally friendly and you don't use up gas. You get fresh air, exercise, and baby naps. Jogging strollers even come in twin designs, and one model is all weather/all terrain.

Infants and napping

You can expect your infant to spend many periods a day catnapping. Again, it counts as sleep. These periods can range from ten minutes to as long as two hours. Some babies eat, are alert, then get irritable and maybe eat again, and finally sleep for a short while. Sometimes there may be one or two periods a day when they sleep for two to three hours, and then they may not catnap at all. As the baby gets older, sleep will become more normalized. Some babies will nap briefly twice a day, while others take just one long nap. It's very common for babies to take one nap in the morning, and then an afternoon siesta, and finally sleep through the night once they reach four to six months.

Change in sleeping patterns

Big changes in your baby's sleeping patterns occur at about five to six months, or when the infant has doubled his birth weight. It is no longer necessary to feed the baby in the middle of the night. In addition, his sleep/wake brain wave patterns are such that he doesn't wake as easily, and he can now sleep for increasingly longer periods. It's possible for a baby to sleep from 8 P.M. to 6 A.M. or so. If it fits your lifestyle for your baby to be up a little longer, you can feed him at 11 P.M., but that doesn't guarantee the baby will sleep later; often they still wake up at 6 A.M. (Don't ask me why.)

"It's bedtime"

You can't expect to put your baby in her crib and she'll just give up waking for sleeping. You need to let the baby know that it's bedtime. You might dim the lights, pull the shades, and generally quiet the house. You are sending a message that it's now sleep time. You might even try saying out loud, "Now we're going to sleep, little one."

You want to develop a bedtime ritual that is different from naptime. Have a firm idea in your mind how long it should last, probably about 20 minutes. Babies can tune in to your vibrations. If you don't have an endpoint to the ritual, your baby won't have an endpoint either.

Climate control

Windows should be open at all times. Not wide open, but at least a crack open in almost any weather. Babies need circulating air. Which brings us to air conditioners. Assuming it's hot and you want an air conditioner on, then it's fine for baby. And it's particularly good for a child with asthma or allergies—especially in allergy season. Obviously, don't let the air blow directly on him at too high a volume. (*Note:* It's a myth that if you blow cold air on a baby he will get a cold.) Keeping a window open is also an important safety measure: Toxic fumes and germs cannot escape if the window is shut.

Do the ritual over and over again

The ritual might be two lullabies, one cuddle-kiss, and a trip around the room saying goodnight to the various stuffed animals and dolls. After a while, the baby will come to expect that ritual. Do it over and over. Don't worry—your baby won't get bored.

Nothing is too silly or childish. I know lawyers who read legal briefs out loud to their infants. Puts them both to asleep.

When the ritual is over

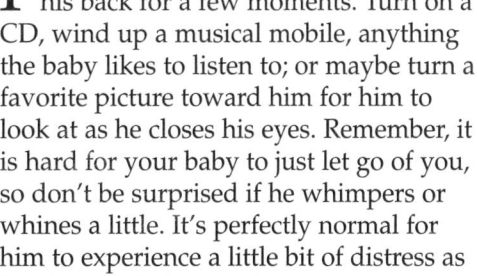

Put the baby in his crib and rub or pat his back for a few moments. Turn on a CD, wind up a musical mobile, anything the baby likes to listen to; or maybe turn a favorite picture toward him for him to look at as he closes his eyes. Remember, it is hard for your baby to just let go of you, so don't be surprised if he whimpers or whines a little. It's perfectly normal for him to experience a little bit of distress as he gives up being awake.

Interestingly, a baby who is put down before he is fast asleep cries less during the night.

Rituals: Both parents take part

Make sure that both Mom and Dad routinely take part in putting the baby to bed. Some children prefer one parent over the other at bedtime. In those families, it is best if the two parents have completely *different* rituals—the baby may become interested in a piece of the ritual of the less-preferred parent that makes it more interesting. That's better than the baby crying for the parent she prefers.

Side sleeping

Not all babies are willing to sleep on their back—now the preferred position. Some may prefer to sleep on their side. Side sleeping allows the infant to easily move into the fetal position, which may help comfort a fussy baby and lessen the possibility of him startling himself awake with his own movements. Extending the baby's lower arm straight out from his body will help stabilize him in the side position and help reduce the chances of him rolling onto his stomach if he moves.

Do a safety check

The first time you respond to a cry, make sure the baby's leg is not caught between the crib slats, and touch the baby's body to make sure she is not feverish. Then come back at five-minute intervals. Don't be surprised if this has to be reinforced every few months. Your child easily forgets the routine and probably hopes that *you* forget the routine as well.

Less is best

If you have to go back into your infant's room because he is still crying, do as little as possible. Say almost nothing. ("Shh. Go back to sleep.") Briefly reassure the baby you are there. Don't give him a bottle, and never pick up the baby unless you want him to get up. (Maybe your husband just got home from a long trip and hasn't seen the baby.) Whatever you do when you "visit," you will inevitably have to do it again and again. If you pick him up, he will cry until you come back and pick him up again. If you reward the baby for waking up by playing with him, he has no good reason to go back to sleep or to stay asleep.

The five-minute rule

As long as the baby continues to cry, continue to check in at five-minute intervals. Each time, wait five minutes, then go back and do the same as before. From this point on, go into your baby's room every five minutes until he falls asleep. You are going in just to reassure him that you have not abandoned him and to repeat the message: It's time to sleep. The time it takes to settle him down should decrease each night.

The goal is not to have the baby feel abandoned. You want him to be thinking, "I guess you don't want to play. You keep coming back and saying '*Ssh.*' I may as well go to sleep."

You'll notice I don't believe in increasing the amount of time it takes to get you to come back in, as do some other books. Behavior modification studies show that if you intermittently reinforce something, or make the reinforcement take longer, you will be positively reinforcing the behavior. *Translation*: If you stretch out the intervals of your return, your baby learns to cry even longer so that you will come.

Middle of the night

What if your baby goes to bed easily at eight in the evening, but then wakes up at two in the morning? Simple. Reread the previous rule. You are in the same situation you would be in if he had trouble going to sleep in the first place. Again, do as little as possible when you enter the room. Don't reinforce his waking up, and he can be taught to go back to sleep. It should take up to a week to get a five-to six-month-old baby to adapt to a more adult sleeping pattern and to be convinced that going to sleep and staying asleep can be a pleasant experience.

Put a piece of your clothing in the crib

Remove your T-shirt in the middle of the night and put it into her crib for comfort. If you have been wearing it for a few hours, it should carry your scent—that's essential. For safety's sake, we are talking about a small piece of light-weight clothing—not a tie or anything a six-month-old can get tangled in.

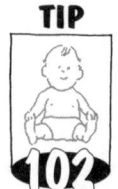

Do not rock baby to sleep in your arms

Do not rock your child to sleep in your arms while listening to music, and then put her into her own bed. When the baby wakes in the middle of the night, she will expect music and rocking in order to get back to sleep. Over the age of six months, you are trying to teach her not to need your arms—except in emergencies, when anything goes. And when you do rock, you want to calm her until she is sleepy but not asleep. So put her down while she is nodding off, eyes fluttering, clearly almost, but not quite, gone.

White noise

Use a white noise machine that plays wave music and other soothing sounds. One parent I know has a sound machine that has eight sounds, including heartbeats. It helps drown out the noises of the day *and* night. If you are questioning the use of white noise, consider that many psychiatrists play white noise in their offices. They use it to block out any noises made by "waiters" and drown out the (possible) "wailers."

Some people use vacuum cleaner sounds. Or you could use a small fan. You can even purchase CDs that reproduce and play white noise. Two recommended recordings are: "Smart Baby's Colic Stop" (888-STOPCRY) and "For Crying Out Loud" (800-548-8531).

Never wake a baby <u>except</u> when he is asleep in the car

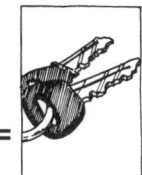

Let me make this clear: It is never, ever acceptable to leave a sleeping baby (or child of any age) alone in a car. Anywhere. Anytime. I've had parents say: "I didn't want to wake him, so I left him safely fastened in his car seat, and I locked the door so nobody could take him, and I left the window open a little and I turned the engine off so he couldn't get carbon monoxide poisoning." You should never do it! Not even in your own driveway or garage. You never know when you leave the baby exactly when you are going to come back. Maybe you go into your house and the phone rings and suddenly minutes have passed—and maybe the car in the driveway wasn't left in park, or the keys are visible, or…. I'm sure you can come up with a dozen worst-case scenarios.

Needless to say, this all goes double for leaving a sleeping child in a car on the street.

Does baby need a humidifier?

I'm often asked if baby needs a humidifier at night. The simple answer is, if baby has a cold, then yes, absolutely. But under normal circumstances, you don't need to have a humidifier on every night for a healthy child. On the other hand, if you live in an apartment or anyplace that has too much steam heat coming up through radiators, then you may wake up in the morning dry and with a sore throat. You need to add more humidity to your child's room. If you have a precrawling baby, then you can just put pans of water around the room—it works just as well. With a crawling child you need a cool-mist humidifier. Avoid hot vaporizers as they provide too good a breeding ground for nasty organisms to grow, and if accidentally tipped over, can actually cause a burn.

Caution: You must clean the humidifier every day to prevent germs from accumulating and being showered all over your baby. Otherwise, it's better not to use it at all.

TIP

Watch for signs of sleepiness

Sometimes baby announces he is tired by rubbing his eyes or sucking his fingers. If you don't look for these signs, your baby can be overtired by the time you figure it out. So lower the lights, turn on the mobile, and put him in his crib at the first telltale signs.

Put infant on a machine that vibrates

In the same vein as a rocking infant seat, put your child on top of a washing machine or dishwasher. Unfortunately you have to turn it *on* for it to work. So your electricity bill may go up while vibrations rock baby to sleep or at least slow him down. Obviously, the baby cannot be left unattended, so just do your wash at the same time. Keep the lights dimmed.

Rocking chair

It's been around for a long time, but don't overlook your basic, standard-issue rocking chair. Baby can be rocked and you don't have to be on your feet. Just sit in a rocking chair and, well, rock. If you don't have one, look for one at a garage sale. Rock, not into deep sleep, but only to "sleepy," and then move baby on to the crib. Remember, if you rock her totally to sleep, you will be stuck doing that over and over. Each time she wakes, she will be wondering what happened to the great rocking chair.

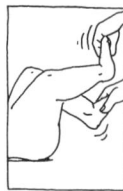

Massage baby's feet

Babies enjoy this as much as adults do. It's been shown to slow down the breathing and heart rate of baby—which is essential for falling asleep. Apply pressure to the bottom of each foot. Make sure your nails are cut down short. (If your nails are long, then use a new pencil head eraser to push in at the bottoms of baby's feet.) The Japanese use foot massage, Shiatsu, to relieve general stress and cure insomnia. Sounds good to me.

Sing "Over in the Meadow"

Pediatrician Julian Orenstein, author of *365 Ways to Calm Your Crying Baby*, swears that this song worked like magic dust for his three children.

Over in the meadow, in the sand, in the sun
Lived an old mother frog and her little froggie one.
Croak! said the mother, I croak, said the one,
So they croaked and were happy in the sand, in the sun

Over in the meadow, in the pond so blue,
Lived an old mother fish and her little fishes two.
Swim! said the mother, We swim, said the two,
So they swam and were happy in the pond so blue.

Over in the meadow, in the nest in the tree,
Lived an old mother bird and her little birdies three.
Sing! said the mother, We sing, said the three,
So they sang and were happy in the nest in the tree.

Play Enya

Anyone who has heard her can back me up on this one. Trust me. She is the perfect combination of sounds of nature—running water, rain, low rolling thunder—with a high-pitched, wordless voice. She puts me right to sleep. She is also regularly used as background music in massage parlors the world over.

Take a bath for two

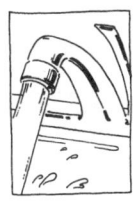

With or without a rubber ducky, a bath is often a part of bedtime rituals for good reason. Dim the lights and fill the tub with warm water just below your breast, and let baby "float" on you. Bathtubs are slippery places, so this needs a partner. You must have another pair of arms to hand the baby over to so you won't have to stand up with a baby in your arms. Besides, if your partner enters the scene to help out, you could end up with a few minutes alone to soak.

3-12 MONTHS: INFANTS

Play a metronome

Set up a metronome on andante cadence. It always put me to sleep in the midst of my music lessons. Make sure the rhythm is not too slow or too fast. If you don't have a metronome, maybe you have a Native American drum. No drum? Find an empty flowerpot. It's the repetition that counts.

Warm the sheets in the dryer

This produces a cozy warmth that is reminiscent of the time baby spent in the womb. Just be careful not to overheat the sheets. This is good for newborns, but it is also applicable to older children when there is a slight nip in the air.

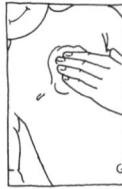

Find the sleep trigger spots

The Japanese claim there are specific sleep trigger spots on the head and neck. Practitioners of Shiatsu and acupuncture also claim certain locations are good for sleep. Gently stroke the soft spot over the fontanel on the top of the head. These trigger spots also correspond to the spots where adults relieve tension headaches. For all we know, babies get headaches and can't tell us. Just gently rub different areas of the head and neck until you find the spots that seem to work for your baby.

Crying baby: Is her formula too strong?

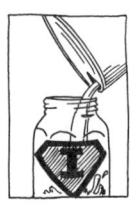

If you are using powder or concentrate, sometimes mixing it in the middle of the night can cause the formula to be off. A simple error can lead to making the formula too strong, which can give baby an upset stomach at the very least. So mix the formula *before* you put your baby to sleep. Always put the water in the bottle first so you can accurately measure out the 8 ounces of water. If you put the powder in first, it's not so easy to tell how much water equals the 8 ounces. Often you end up putting in less water than needed, and then it's too concentrated.

Close your eyes

We know that babies can imitate adults. If you stick your tongue out, they often stick their tongue out—it's like a mirror. Whatever it takes to calm a baby is worth trying. It's not so different from the hypnosis "trick" where you tell people they are getting sleepy and guess what? They get sleepy. So close your eyes, this shouldn't be too difficult for you!

Yawn a lot

As you've probably observed, yawning is downright contagious. Just try it in a room full of adults—you can practically pass the yawn around the room like playing a game of telephone. This works the same with babies.

Sleeptime for children with asthma and allergies

The environment a child sleeps in has a great impact on a child with asthma or allergies. Some children have symptoms of asthma as early as six months.

Children with asthma should never sleep with feather bedding. Give away all those lovely down blankets. The bedding should always be 100 percent cotton—no blends or mixtures. What she breathes in has a great effect on her, so you have to pay particular attention to all those hours she is just lying in her crib. If she breathes in dust from the floor around the crib, she will be doing it all night long, and that is one reason why most asthmatic attacks occur during the night.

TIP

120

Is it health related?

If sleep is interrupted suddenly, consider that it may be health related.

It could be anything from a cold to an ear infection or teething—and there are solutions for each one. Obviously you may get daytime clues that the child has an illness that could pop up at bedtime. Consider the "cures" before even putting baby to bed and be prepared to handle them if necessary during the night.

If a parent comes home late, don't wake baby up to play

A parent who comes home late may naturally want to play with baby. There's a real temptation to wake the baby, but it's not a good habit to get into. It interferes with sleep training and excites the baby. But that doesn't mean Mom or Dad can't take part in sleep rituals: they can "be" a warm fuzzy by letting baby cuddle with them. The late parent could be the one to take a bath with baby.

Reinforce sleep training

Infants sometimes begin to wake and cry for *you*. They are beginning to understand that you exist even when they don't actually see you. When baby can find "hidden" objects is about the time of separation anxiety. It's time to reteach baby to go back to sleep. (Reread tip #100, "The five-minute rule.")

Tolerate noise

Help your child become accustomed to noise by having a reasonably noisy household in the background when he naps and sleeps. Don't be on guard to make your home super quiet. Run the vacuum cleaner if you must. Let your child learn to develop a tolerance for noises. If your child is aware everyone else is up and having fun, he will want to join in. Don't appear to be having too much fun.

Teething

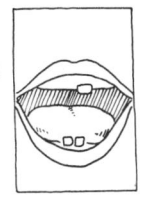

Teething accounts for frequent night waking in babies age three to four months. However, you may not *see* the first tooth until 6 to 8 months or even as late as 18 months. You can usually tell by baby's crying, biting, ear tugging, rash around lips, hand in mouth, and profuse drooling. Despite what your mother or your next-door neighbor tells you, teething does *not* cause fever. But it can cause misery. For nighttime, when baby shouldn't be chewing on a frozen bagel (which works wonders during the day), pain medicine in recommended doses can help. For children six months or older, try any teething gel and apply directly to the gums. For really difficult teethers, consult your doctor for a prescription-strength teething gel that dentists use, which really numbs the gums.

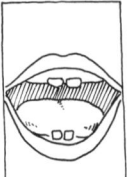

Teething, part II

For teething, some parents like herbal alternatives. One mother in my practice swears by sweet brake, an herb touted for its soothing effect. If herbal remedies appeal to you, take a stroll to your local health food store when your baby isn't crying. Or just browse on the Web for healthy alternatives, but always check with your baby's doctor before using.

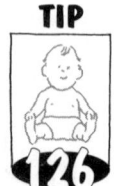

Sing "Good Night Irene"

If friends are around, do it in harmony. This is the perfect song, of course, if your baby happens to be named Irene or another name that easily fits in, like Diane. The idea is to take poetic license. If you recall, in the movie *Three Men and a Baby*, those particular three men would gather around the baby's crib and sing "Good Night Sweetheart" over and over until she went off to sleep.

Read or sing Lullaby and Goodnight: Songs for Sweet Dreams

This wonderful book by Julie Downing (Simon & Schuster, 1999), contains the personal favorites of the author/illustrator. She says, "I remember the feeling of comfort and safety when my mother sang to me. After my own children were born I wanted to share some favorite lullabies with them." Falling asleep, as we've noted, can be difficult for young children, and a lullaby smoothes the transition between bedtime and sleep.

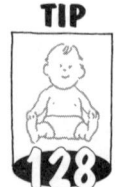

TIP 128

3-12 MONTHS: INFANTS

Sing "Hush, Little Baby"

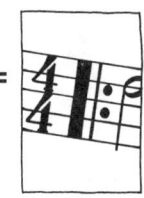

This is a really popular lullaby—the title says it all! Almost anyone knows the first verse, but in case just one verse won't do, here's two, and more.

Hush, little baby, don't say a word,
Mama's gonna buy you a mockingbird.
And if that mockingbird don't sing,
Mama's gonna buy you a diamond ring.
And if that diamond ring turns brass,
Mama's gonna buy you a looking glass.
And if that looking glass gets broke,
Mama's gonna buy you a billy goat.
And if that billy goat won't pull,
Mama's gonna buy you a cart and bull.
And if that cart and bull turn over,
Mama's gonna buy you a dog named Rover.
And if that dog named Rover won't bark,
Mama's gonna buy you a horse and cart.
And if that horse and cart fall down,
You'll still be the sweetest little baby in town.

Don't run in too soon

You shouldn't run in too quickly to attend to the first cry of your older infant. But you can run in at the *second* cry. The more quickly parents attend to slight cries and movements, the more the baby becomes accustomed to short sleeps and frequent rousings. This is why intercom monitors can be hazardous to your baby's sleep.

Just say no...to water beds

Never put an infant to sleep, or leave an infant unattended, on a water bed. She can suffocate in the facedown position or roll between the mattress and frame. Your preschooler might enjoy a "ride" on a water bed, but even she should not be sleeping on one. Reserve water beds as an adult-only pleasure.

Stick to your bedtime

Don't postpone an infant's sleep to make a relative or grandmother happy. A sleepy child kept awake just becomes irritable and is too wound up to settle down. Remember, problems at night spill over into disruptive days. Grandma will still be there in the morning, and she'll be well rested. Otherwise, she could be up all night, if the baby was kept up past bedtime.

TIP

3-12 MONTHS: INFANTS

All bets are off if your infant is sick

A good sleeper can temporarily become a bad one if she has a tummy ache, an ear infection, or a high fever. Then you have to hold, rock, and comfort her and do whatever needs doing to solve the problem at hand. Bring her into your room or stay with her in hers, but make sure you *both* understand this is temporary. Say to her, "Tomorrow you will sleep just fine."

Question: "Why is it that the later my baby goes to bed, the earlier he wakes up?"

This question doesn't have a universal answer. What seems to be true is that when people are overtired, their sleep cycle is disturbed. That means they often wake up under stimuli that wouldn't ordinarily wake them. So let's say you are supposed to be in a deep sleep cycle in the middle of the night and a fire engine goes blaring by the window. Most times you won't wake up. But tonight you went to bed very late and you are not in a really deep sleep when that fire engine passes. You are in a light cycle and wake up. Even for babies, being overtired disrupts and alters the sleep cycle, which results in disordered sleep and disordered waking as well. In the case of a baby, as soon as the sun starts to shine through her windows, she can be stimulated to wake up if she is not in a deep-enough sleep.

TIP

What's a good bedtime?

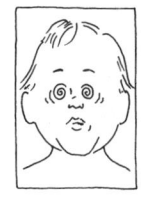

A good bedtime for a 4- to 12-month-old is 6 to 8 P.M. Parents often get used to kids who are cranky and irritable late in the day, and don't think of putting them to bed soon enough. What you have come to see as normal behavior may actually be a child who is overtired.

Wake-up time

Don't go in to a crying baby too soon in the morning. If you go in *too* early, she may get up earlier and earlier just for the pleasure of your company. The first time you do go in, if you just soothe her or give her a rattle or something to play with, she may go back to sleep.

Note: If you hear her happily cooing, just let her coo away. Don't feel the need to join in the conversation. Respect her right to talk to herself.

Head banging

Some children bang their heads in their cribs. They never injure themselves. About 5 to 10 percent of infants bang or roll their head before sleep. This behavior often starts at about eight months, or when the child starts to crawl, and is more common in boys. Although this behavior is generally normal, some parents panic and think of serious conditions such as autism. If your baby's behavior is otherwise normal, don't worry about it. Head banging seems to be another version of self-pacifying; some children find that rhythmic rocking feels good as well.

Massage

Massage is wonderful as long as it is age appropriate. For the first six months of life, baby should be lying on her back. For the child six months and older, you can have her lie on her stomach and massage upper back and thighs, or push legs up to "froggy" position and massage lower back. A nice back rub is always appreciated. Use your thumbs in an upward, outward motion, pressing down firmly enough to just move the skin. You don't want it to be so light that you tickle the baby—which will just wake her up into a giggle. Always take your lead from the baby's response. A baby whose eyes are closing is a good sign for you to continue doing exactly what you are doing. If baby cries or is agitated, then it's time to stop. Remember, your goal is to get your baby sleepy.

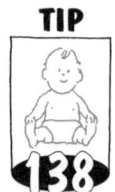

3-12 MONTHS: INFANTS

Massage, part II

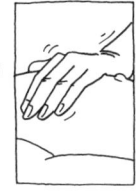

The room should be warm, since the child should be undressed, and the lights dimmed. (Play a soothing tape for your listening pleasure.) After six months of age, you can use a lightweight baby oil on your baby. Make sure your hands are moist and almost slippery. Avoiding the baby's head, apply oil gently all over. At some point in the next twelve hours, make sure the baby is bathed so that the oil doesn't clog her pores. Obviously, don't give the baby a bath right after the massage or she will wake up!

Tips for international adoption

Multicultural awareness is a good way to approach making your newly adopted child more comfortable at sleeptime. Today we realize that even in utero the baby has some sense of sound and smell. (Sounds and smells can definitely have a calming impact on a baby.) You have to consider what your baby was accustomed to before she was adopted. Use fragrances (herbs) and cooking odors of her culture of origin. Put pictures of people of her culture of origin in her crib: You want to comfort her at night with what she is familiar with.

Adoption continued: Does baby need company?

Your baby might need to have people around him because that is what he is used to. Your infant may be used to sleeping in a group setting, particularly if he lived in an orphanage. Simulate his early memories by moving his crib into your room, or even consider a family bed. You should acknowledge where he came from by re-creating his environment of origin to some extent.

Adoption continued: Sing lullaby in baby's language of origin

In my practice, I examined beautiful Zara, who was of Mandarin descent. At 15 months, Zara, who had been adopted from China, was sullen, silent. Her adoptive parents tried everything they could think of, but there was no change until they acquired a tape of Mandarin Chinese lullabies. Not only did Zara sleep better, but she began to smile and babble and soon was talking in both languages.

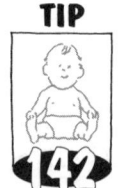

Infants and traveling

A word about jet lag: If you have a choice, infants should fly at night. Babies adjust best if they don't get overtired, even if we do. If you are flying *east*, expect a longer midday nap, but don't let it last too long, or you will miss your chance to get a good first night's sleep after arrival.

3-12 MONTHS: INFANTS

Daylight saving time

Don't forget about daylight saving time, which can play havoc with sleeping schedules. (Even your dog may be off.) Going into spring (when the clock springs forward an hour), it's best to keep baby up an extra half hour the evening after the clocks change. Going into fall (when the clock falls back) your baby may not be tired at her usual bedtime. So cut out her afternoon nap or shorten it the first day or two after you change clocks, so she can fall asleep at the "new" bedtime (an hour earlier to her body clock). Sometimes, out of frustration, I just pretended the time didn't change. I would just ignore daylight saving time.

Treating baby's cold

If a cold is interfering with sleep, you can "steam" a newborn or infant for a brief period—that is, turn the water on in the shower very hot and bring the baby into the bathroom (but **NOT** into the shower!) to breathe in the steam. Don't steam for more than one minute or two at a time. Keep the bathroom door half-open to prevent heat damage to baby's lungs. You can also put several drops of saline in each of baby's nostrils and use a cool-mist humidifier, but avoid eucalyptus with newborns.

Colds continued: Elevate baby

Elevate mattress slightly when baby has a cold. Of course this doesn't work with a newborn or smaller infant, they just slide down. Do not put a pillow under baby's head. Instead, roll up a towel and place it under the head of the mattress. When I was a resident, I worked in a hospital that had a special "peg" bed for babies who had reflux—that is, food comes up from the stomach. We would arrange them on an angled board with the peg between the legs. We would just "hang" the baby on the board. That's really what you need! I saw one of these at a Juvenile Product Manufacturers Association annual convention, but I admit I have not seen one get to the commercial market yet. Now there's an idea.

Just say no... to cold medicines

Never give cold medicine to a child under six months of age, and then only with your doctor's approval. When you *do* give cold medicine, choose one with a single ingredient, like one meant just to calm a cough. Unfortunately, today it's rare to find single-ingredient cold medicines. Some combinations can be disastrous. Understand that there is a potential for side effects with all medicines—the more ingredients, the greater the chance for side effects. I also say *diagnose before you dose.* (So if your child has fever and a cough, don't use a medicine that says it's for "sore throat and a stuffed nose.")

Treating baby's gas

Chamomile tea does wonders for gas, but give the tea as the last liquid about an hour before sleep. With baby lying on his belly on a firm surface and his legs in froggy position, you can firmly massage his lower back in counterclockwise movements. You can also put the well-lubricated tip of a rectal thermometer into the anus to get some gas release.

Just say no...to simethicone

Simethicone is an antigas medication that is supposedly not absorbed by the intestinal tract. In some children, it sedates not only the intestines but the nervous system as well, and the child becomes lethargic. When this happens, it can look as though the child is very sick, when what he really is is drugged.

The medicine cabinet for infants

Here are some suggestions of items to keep in your medicine cabinet.

- chamomile tea bags
- infant versions of Tylenol and Motrin (be sure of child's weight)
- teething gel
- cold medicine (single ingredient)
- Vaseline
- rectal thermometer (with Vaseline on tip can be used to relieve distended belly of child with constipation or gas)

Sing "Alice the Camel"

This is one of those nice repetitive songs that works to the tune of "One Little, Two Little, Three Little Indians."

Alice the camel has five humps,
Alice the camel has five humps,
Alice the camel has five humps,
So go, Alice, go.

Alice the camel has four humps,
Alice the camel has four humps,
Alice the camel has four humps,
So go, Alice, go.

Alice the camel has three humps,
Alice the camel has three humps,
Alice the camel has three humps,
So go, Alice, go.

Sing each verse again as:
Alice the camel has two humps;
Alice the camel has one hump;
Alice the camel has no humps (but the last line is now changed to:)
Now Alice is a horse.

TIP

3-12 MONTHS: INFANTS

Be prepared

When you are dealing with an ill child, I always recommend you come armed and prepared. What that means is you don't want to come into the room evaluating and assessing. Try to figure out in advance how you will treat the baby. Don't start fumbling in the dark. So if your child is teething, you should come in with one finger covered in teething gel and a prefilled dropper of Tylenol in the other hand. If your child has a cold, then in one hand you have a prefilled syringe with saline and in the other, a dropper full of cold medicine. You don't want to walk in with bottles that can be spilled or suddenly realize you can't find the cap; then you have to put on the light to make sure you didn't drop it in her crib!

Blackout shades

Some babies at six months do need pitch-dark, and you may have to buy blackout shades to block out the early morning sunlight. If your baby is light sensitive, then install heavy shades. Come in in the morning, lift the blinds to let in the sunlight, and announce, "It's time to get up."

Family bed

There are different arrangements for "sharing sleep" with children. One way is to bring baby right into bed with you. This often works for breastfeeding mothers. If you admit that your child is in bed with you, you may hear another parent say, "My baby sleeps with me, too, but don't tell anyone." It's not uncommon; it's just not talked about. (This is changing somewhat as the family bed achieves a renewed respectability. So listen up.)

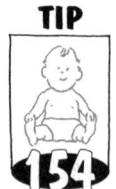

Sleeping arrangements: "Sidecar"

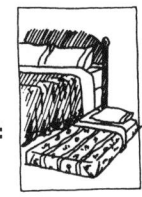

Some parents like a "sidecar" arrangement. The baby is not in your bed but close by. Remove one side rail from the crib and place the crib next to your bed. Make sure to adjust the crib mattress level to the exact level of your mattress; but there should be no space between your mattress and baby's crib. If the crib is on wheels, be sure they are in the locked position. There actually exists a commercially made sidecar bassinet that ensures there is no gap between your bed and your baby's.

Safe sleep position, revisited

Older infants who are able to move by themselves should never be physically restrained in order to force them to sleep on their backs. An older infant who is used to sleeping on her stomach may be resistant to change. If parents are concerned, they can let the tummy sleeper fall asleep on her stomach first, and then switch her, or hold and rock her to sleep before putting her down. (*Warning:* You will be doing this repeatedly.) Do not get up during the night and continually switch baby onto her back.

However, if you have any family history of SIDS, if baby was premature, or if the baby has any cardiac or pulmonary disease, if she won't sleep on her back, you may *have* to turn her over. Consult your doctor.

Wean baby from early morning feedings

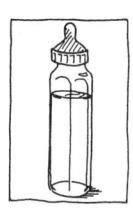

You can wean baby from the early morning feeding. Children over the age of five months do not need to be fed at the break of dawn. In my book, if it's dark, it's night, and that means sleep time. Reinforce that there is no feeding until the lights come up. I have a mother in my practice whose child was not thriving, not gaining enough weight. She had to interfere with her child's sleep by feeding her when she woke up at 4:30 in the morning. As soon as her daughter regained weight, over a two-week period, I said, "Okay, let's sleep train again. No more waking up to feed in the morning." The mom replied, "God bless you, but I was going to do that anyway."

Desperate measures: Nurse until you both fall asleep

You can do this only for a short period of time, but sometimes desperate times call for desperate measures. If you absolutely need to sleep, and you are nursing, just put a blanket down on the floor, and nurse baby.

Warning: You may awake with a raw nipple.

Sing "Keemo Kymo"

Here's an unusual lullaby handed down from a pediatrician. Make up any tune you like—just make sure it's soothing.

There was a frog lived in a spring
Sing song kitty catcha ky-mee-oh
He could dance and he could sing
Sing song kitty catchy kymee-oh

Keeme kymo dayro dime
Hey, ho, subble bubble sipso
Perwinkle soapfat, pennywinkle nip cat
Kitty catcha kymee-oh

Oh, what you gonna do when the rain don't fall?
Sing song kitty catcha kymee-oh
Crops grow small instead of tall
Sing song kitty catcha kymee-oh

Keemo kymo dayro dime
Hey, ho, subble bubble sipso
Perwinkle soapfat, pennywinkle nip cat
Kitty catchy kymee-oh

3-12 MONTHS: INFANTS

Avoid caffeine

Don't give products with caffeine to your child. Similarly, avoid coffee, chocolate, and colas if you are breastfeeding. Children show markedly different sensitivities to caffeine, which acts as a stimulant. It can easily interfere with sleep by prolonging the time needed to fall asleep, and it disrupts sleep stages, which leads to more frequent wakeups.

Tea time

Give your child Sleepytime tea or chamomile tea. The warmth alone will help him unwind. But don't assume that *all* herb teas are appropriate for babies. Many herbal teas actually contain caffeine or other active ingredients that are innocuous for adults but could have toxic effects in babies. Stay away from poorly or unlabeled substances.

Sleeping arrangements: The extended bed

Put the crib mattress on the floor next to your bed. This allows the child to wean from the family bed. Make sure there is no space between the mattress and your bed or your baby could roll off and underneath it. This is a good transition if the child has been in your bed for a period of time.

Identical twins

Identical twins, not surprisingly, sleep more *alike* than fraternal twins do. Twins have spent nine months together listening to the same heartbeat and swimming in the same gene pool, so whether they are identical or fraternal, they often like to sleep in the same crib. Put them down to sleep at the same time, and cross your fingers.

TIP 163

Fraternal twins

Most parents instinctively let fraternal twins sleep in the same crib until they start fighting, which is at about 18 months. This holds true even if the twins are different sexes. I joke that twins can sleep together until there is bloodshed. You might want to separate them if one twin is sick, but chances are good that they will be sick together anyway.

Simulate a baby's bedroom

One of my parents came up with a novel idea when one twin, the boy, had sleep problems. She wanted the boy to stay in his own crib while dealing with his sleep training. She remembered the rule that it's not a good idea to go to sleep in one place and wake in another, so she used a little corner of the living room to re-create the bedroom. She simulated the children's room, using the same sheets and mobile, and transferred the sleeping *girl* twin as soon as she was asleep. This way, if the girl woke, she was in familiar surroundings.

Read (or sing) <u>Sleep, Sleep, Sleep: A Lullaby for Little Ones Around the World</u>

This book, *Sleep, Sleep, Sleep: A Lullaby for Little Ones Around the World*, by Nancy Van Laan, pictures by Holly Meade (Little Brown, 1995), contains lullabies from all around the world—from China to Norway and all seven continents.

TIP 166

3-12 MONTHS: INFANTS

Parent-to-parent: The white wall

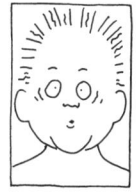

I discovered that my babies, from age two months to about six months, calmed when I took them into our very small bathroom and held them gently against my chest in such a position that they could look at the blank white wall. It seemed to me that the overstimulation of a long day was hard to let go of, so the visual blankness of the wall enabled them to soothe themselves.

12-36 Months: **Toddlers**

FYI: Toddlers resist bedtime

At about two years, a child with a perfectly good sleep track record may begin to resist bedtime and become afraid of the dark and have nightmares. This is about the same time they have difficulty separating from you. So you have to help them with the transition from enjoying you, to enjoying being in their room—independent from you. Sleep training may need to be reinforced again.

Don't feed toddler solids close to bedtime

Don't give your toddler dinner at 9 P.M., thinking she'll sleep better. Having a full tummy at bedtime is an invitation to a stomachache. If she eats too much at night, she can have trouble falling asleep. Remember, though, that toddlers try to delay going to sleep, so they may ask for a snack. If you must give a bedtime snack, offer Jell-O or applesauce, not ice cream or a Twinkie.

Bedroom door open

There are two distinct schools of thought on whether to keep the bedroom door open or shut. In the open-door corner: Parents always leave the door slightly ajar, if for no other reason than to be reassured themselves. Kids in open-door rooms are often somewhat afraid of the dark, in part because of shadows they have watched throughout their early years. Often, all these children need is a night-light or flashlight. Obviously, an open-door seems like an invitation to come on out.

Bedroom door shut

In the closed-door corner: Babies are put to sleep in the dark, usually with a monitor. It is believed that a child who has learned to sleep in the dark with the door closed is a child who will never be afraid of the dark and is therefore better off. By the time the child is a toddler, the door is a natural barrier that helps establish boundaries.

Never lock the door or threaten to hold it shut as a punishment.

Let your child wish on a star

Many parents have turned their child's ceiling into a twinkling sky using glow-in-the-dark stars. At night you can take turns wishing on one. You make the wish for the little one until she is old enough. Why not sing "Twinkle, Twinkle Little Star"?

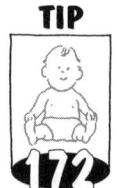

Put your children in the same room

Instead of having your kids sleep in separate rooms, try bunking them in the same room. It's likely that they will comfort each other to sleep. Studies show that children under three sleep better sharing a bedroom. In the same vein, older children can help put younger siblings to sleep. Many of my parents tell me that an older sibling will read or sing their sibling to sleep. (My older brother had his own method of keeping me quiet. If I made noise at bedtime, he would throw his shoe at me from across the room. I don't recommend it, but it sure worked.)

Toddlers and colds

It's hard to sleep with a stuffed nose, and an infant with a cold is cranky enough. If your toddler has a cold, steam her in the bathroom for five minutes before putting her to sleep. Turn the hot shower on full blast, and close the bathroom door until the steam builds up. Then, stand inside the bathroom (not the shower) with the baby for five minutes to loosen the congestion. The baby should be wrapped in a towel, not pj's, because she is bound to get sweaty and wet. If she is asleep by the time you finish, just put her down without pj's.

Just say no...to your toddler sleeping with you

It's not unusual for two-year-olds to resist going to bed, and then later to wake up and insist on getting into their parents' bed. At some point, you may decide that you are no longer going to take your toddler into bed with you. You may at first be rewarded with crying. Toddlers resist staying in their own beds because they enjoy a tremendous amount of closeness with their parents at this age, and they are not yet good at calming themselves down at night after a hectic day. Don't back down. And when you consider the family bed in the first place, if baby isn't going to be welcome when she is bigger and more active, you might be better off kicking her out of your bed before toddlerhood.

Enjoy your toddler during the day

Make sure you spend time enjoying your toddler during the day. This way, not only will you have fun with your toddler, but at night you won't feel guilty that you need to spend more time with your child. If you are a working parent, try making some time in the morning for playtime. Just be sure your toddler has plenty of outdoor time for fresh air and exercise.

Bedtime ritual, revisited

Develop a new bedtime ritual with your toddler that makes bedtime as pleasant as possible. Maybe each night there can be bath time followed by some gentle massage time, and then it's tea and two stories. The routine can be anything you want as long as it helps your child feel more relaxed about bedtime.

Toddlers and timers

Timers can announce to children that bedtime has arrived. Children are told that when the timer goes off, it will be time to get ready for bed. In this way, parents are relieved of making this unpopular announcement. For reasons I'm not quite sure of, most kids seem to accept the reality of bedtime when the timer goes off. This helps children learn to control the world with some dignity.

Just say no... to your toddler's being a TV–couch potato

Don't let your toddler fall asleep on the couch watching TV, and then carry her to bed. Again, if she wakes up later in her bed, she is going to expect TV in order to go back to sleep. Studies now suggest that the blue light emitted by the TV stimulates the pineal gland and can cause the child to stay awake.

12-36 MONTHS: TODDLERS

Sleep training: Breaking the crying and waking pattern

While you are sleep training, your baby will go through periods when she gets up and retests you to see if you really mean she has to go back to sleep. During that time you are likely to face some challenging moments. Since *you* may have trouble sleeping as well, you might want to wait for a Friday evening so you won't face work exhausted the next day. If you live in an apartment building, you may want to inform your neighbors that they may hear some crying because you are teaching your toddler to stay in bed. I know of a policeman who showed up at an apartment in the middle of the night because of a screaming baby. When the tired, frazzled parents came to the door, the cop said, "Let me guess—you are trying to Ferberize the baby?" He was referring to the popular sleep book by Dr. Ferber, which advocates a particular version of letting babies cry themselves to sleep. (A method I am not in total agreement with.)

The five-minute rule, revisited

As soon as your toddler cries, wait five minutes before entering his room. Once you go in, quietly reassure him that he must sleep. Lay him back down, stroke his back a few times, and leave. Do not pick him up or give him a bottle. Of course if he feels feverish or is complaining of pain, all bets are off. (See rules for dealing with illnesses.)

Enlist the aid of older siblings

Parents often don't quite know what to do when they are trying to stick to a sleep program with a toddler who shares a room with an older sibling. Parents don't want the older child to be woken up by the toddler and often will just give in to the toddler and even let her sleep in their bed. Let the older child know what you are doing and explain that you need her help. Often, you have to remove the older child from the bedroom because the toddler needs to be returned to her bed or is up crying. Let the older child sleep someplace else in the house—like a couch in the family room or even in a sleeping bag—for a few days. You could even offer her a small reward for helping the family out.

No extras

Just as you did with your infant, make sure your toddler doesn't receive "extras" for being awake. Do not hold and rock him or give him juice. If he gets to play and has your attention, why should he want to go easily back to sleep?

Don't sneak out of your toddler's room

Do not lie down with your child until she falls asleep and then attempt to tiptoe out. If you want to lie down for a few minutes, make sure to leave before she has fallen asleep. If you sneak out of her room, you are setting up a bad pattern. You are just delaying the moment of truth when your child will finally be faced with having to be on her own at bedtime. Besides, she quite reasonably will learn not to trust you.

No falling asleep in your bed

Don't let your child fall asleep in your bed because she doesn't like her own room. This is one more approach that distorts bedtime reality and keeps a youngster from learning how to handle bedtime. This doesn't mean that on rare occasions she can't come in for a special treat. Kids will think of any excuse to get into your bed. One two-year-old claimed she liked her parents' bedding much better than her own. So her parents let her borrow it and put it on *her* bed.

Choosing bedtime and wake-up time

Keep in mind that children differ in how much sleep they require. Your child may be one of those youngsters who doesn't need much sleep. If you have one of these children, you may have to make some choices. You could make bedtime later. Try putting the child down at 10 P.M. and she might sleep through until 6 A.M. Most people would rather be up with the child a little later than be woken up too early. If you choose to put your child to bed earlier, then you and your partner may just have to "spot" each other at getting up at 4 A.M. Looking ahead, encourage your early riser to take up a hobby like reading so you can get back to sleep.

Sharing a room: Same bedtime

Children who are within three years of each other are best put to bed at the same time if they are sharing a bedroom. To help make this work, find a ritual that works for both of them. As much as possible, let them have some of their own independent space—with their input in decorating within the same room. Just because one kid loves Barney doesn't mean the entire bedroom should be plastered with Barney. You can personalize the sleep space with decals or let each one paint the wall next to his or her own bed.

Sharing a room: Different bedtimes

If children are spaced more than three years apart, then they should have separate bedtimes. The older child usually has the later bedtime and this creates no special problem. The youngster rarely awakens when the older child is being put to sleep. Some siblings might as well be called oil and water because they really don't mix. But if there is no alternative because of space constraints, then allow the children to have control over their space. One family in my practice put masking tape down the center of the room to give each child their own territory.

Parent-to-parent: Whisper

"I lie down beside Zane and whisper to him. I talk in a soft whisper about the day and what we will do the next day. I am really quiet. He listens and whispers back. It often puts him to sleep."

The moms at the Web site *www.drpaula.com* are always exchanging tips on sleep. Zane's mom definitely has the right idea. Whenever you are trying to wind a child down, it helps to whisper. That's what I do in my office, especially when dealing with a "wired" child. Just that one act usually brings down the level of anxiety, even if it's in a room full of kids. Some children hone in on the whisperer and wonder why the person is speaking differently. Interestingly, no one reacts to a whispering adult by shouting; they usually whisper back.

Unwind time

At the end of any high-stress day, you need extra time to lead up to the bedtime ritual. You can call this transition anything you want to—just leave space for the unwinding. Even infants can be stressed at times.

We used to have "evenings." This in-between period seems to be getting rarer, but you can reclaim it, if you carve it out and plan for it.

"Stuffed" friends

Every child should have at least one special stuffed animal to sleep with. (You could even put little pajamas on his special friend at night.) This way, the child isn't really sleeping alone. Although your young child may become attached to a special bear or a Cabbage Patch doll or whatever the craze happens to be, even adolescents have been known to (sheepishly) pack these same stuffed friends off to summer camp.

Transitional objects, revisited

Encourage your child's attachment to a "blanky" or "lovey." These transitional objects become substitutes for Mommy or Daddy when they aren't there and help young children tolerate separations. They comfort your child as he makes the transition from dependent baby to less-dependent child. A child who can hug a blanky at night has the satisfaction of feeling as if his parents are close. But be aware that children get very attached to these replacements of you.

Don't sneak out

From newborn on, let your child see you go out the door when you're leaving her. Parents often don't want their little one to get upset knowing that Mom and Dad have left for a while. But young children have to learn to tolerate separation from their parents. If children learn to do this, they are in a better position at night to separate from Mom and Dad and go to bed. Also, they won't be worrying about whether you are really home, and they can trust you.

"Mommy and Daddy": Getting attention

At this age, she can actually call out for "Mommy" or "Daddy," so she is harder to ignore. Reread earlier tips. Especially remember never to get close enough that she can actually grab you through the crib rails. There is nothing worse than peeling a child off your body. It's a little like ripping Velcro. As she gets a little older, you will deal with a child who is even harder to ignore, because she can rattle her cage. Mothers call and say to me, "I don't know what to do because she is crying so hard." I respond, "You don't expect her to cry softly, do you?" Her goal is to wake you up and get some attention. Don't be moved by her intensity—she'll get over it.

Bedtime problems

Make sure bedtime problems and concerns are handled by both parents. There are still some fathers who are convinced that any bedtime problem is a "mom" problem. After all, he has to go to work tomorrow. (As if Mom doesn't work, too!) Moms shouldn't have to jump through hoops to keep the kids quiet so Daddy can get his sleep and not be mad at them. Dad's in this as much as Mom is. Dads are in fact sometimes more successful at sleep matters than moms are. Perhaps this is by virtue of the fact that they are around less often and don't take it all so personally.

TIP 195

12-36 MONTHS: TODDLERS

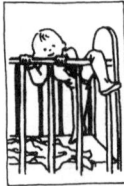

Crawling out of the crib

As soon as a child can crawl out of her crib, you have to change the sleeping arrangements. Some children just have the agility of a monkey and nothing can keep them in their cribs at night—short of Velcro. (Just kidding.) If your baby's nipples come to the top of the rails of the crib when she is standing, then the crib is no longer safe. At this point, she can fling herself over the crib rail. Drill holes, if necessary, in the four legs of the crib and lower the mattress even further. Eventually you may have to remove the rail altogether and teach her how to shimmy out. Also put pillows on the floor to soften the landing in case she topples out.

Time for a real bed

When your child can hoist a leg over the crib rail, it's now time for a *real* bed. Parents have found it helpful to place an approved gate—installed safely—at the doorway of the bedroom so she cannot leave her room when she gets up. Make the bedroom as childproof as possible. Your goal is to keep your youngster in her room without repeatedly catering to her in the middle of the night.

The big bed transition

When it's time to make the transition to a big bed, many parents make the mistake of just dismantling the crib and whisking it away. It's OK for the crib to be empty for a while before the new baby comes, after the older child moves into the big bed. Just keep the crib in the room for a while and use it for toy storage or throw stuffed animals into it. Keep the crib available, not just because the child might regress but so he can be comforted by its presence.

Big bed, part II

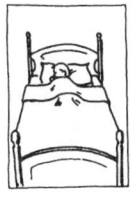

Usually, if a new baby is expected, the older child gets a new bed, and a new baby just appears in the crib. It's not a bad idea to wait a little to move the older child so he doesn't feel displaced. It should be more like a graduation. You can help with the transition by using bedsheets on the big bed similar—at least in color—to those you used in the crib. Then, take your child to pick the sheets and blankets, and focus on what excites your child, not your decorator. This is a significant event.

Read <u>My New Bed: From Crib to Bed</u>

This one, *My New Bed: From Crib to Bed*, by the Berenstains (Random House, 1999), is part of the Berenstain Baby Bears series. It begins: "When I was small, as small as can be, my crib was just right for me." Now the crib is not big enough for all of baby bear's stuff. Most little ones relate well to this scenario and are comforted.

Leaving bed

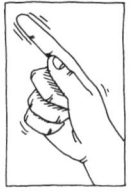

What about the child who leaves his bed? Swiftly and firmly return the older child to his bed and remind him that he belongs in bed. Typically this is ignored the first few times a youngster hears it. Return the youngster to his bed; leave a closet light or night-light on. Count to three and close your eyes and challenge your child to make it back to his bed before you finish counting.

Rely on sitters with older children

With younger children, family members *are* preferable if you can enlist them to sit. A really young child can't tell you how the baby sitter reacts. In general, family members are more patient and less likely to do unacceptable things to your children. For older toddlers and preschoolers, rely occasionally on sitters other than family members. When you leave your child with relatives, you are not truly giving your child the chance to learn how to separate. Family is family, and it's almost like being with Mom and Dad.

Obviously, there are some basic rules that must be followed with sitters. Make sure you have checked out the sitter's references and take the time to introduce her to your child before you go out for the evening. Explain your child's bedtime routine to the sitter. You might also have a neighbor or family member pay a "surprise" call, just to see how things are going. Always leave a number where you can be contacted.

TIP

"Help, there's a child in my bed."

What about the child who sneaks into your room at night and stays in your bed until morning? Parents often say they didn't hear the child come in. (And yes, it is kind of cute.) Place a suitcase or some object against your bedroom door at night. That way the moment your little one tries to sneak in, he will make a banging noise, which will wake you up. Then you take him back to his room. Keep a flashlight by your bed to guide him back. When you return to your bedroom, set up the alarm system again. If you think he might trip over your alarm, you could put a bell on his door, or let the door squeak, or invest in one of those mats that ring when you step on it.

12-36 MONTHS: TODDLERS

The parent chair

Here's a system that works, but it takes a little time, patience, and fortitude. Put a chair outside your child's door. Bring a book to read, a little nightlight for your book, and a pot of coffee. Be prepared to stay. When he toddles out, and he will, turn him around and walk him back to his bed. Say, "I'm right here and I'll stay here as long as you are up. I won't let anything bad happen to you." For a school-age child, you can add a semi-stern: "Get back in bed." Most children will run back to bed if they are caught at the threshold and greeted none too cheerfully. Let your child know you are setting limits.

During the day, reinforce his need to sleep in his own bed

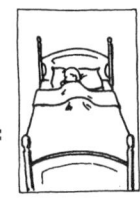

During the day, reinforce the importance of sleeping all night in his own bed. There's a wonderful, charming book, *Llamas in Pajamas* (Gisela Voss and Melissa Sweet, Museum of Fine Arts, Boston, 1995). Read books like that to your child during the *day* so going to sleep becomes part of everyday life. My kids loved me to read, *The Baby Beebee Bird,* by Diane Redfield Massie (Harper & Row, 1963). It is all about tired animals in the zoo and the bird who sang "beebee bobbi bobbi." It ended with the wise words: "Night time is really best for sleeping." But it doesn't have to be nighttime for you to read to your kids.

Play "let's sleep"

During the day, you can play act. Make-believe is fun for children. In this case, play "let's go to sleep." Let your child put *you* to sleep. The toddler can put a blanket around you, "read," and kiss you. This is all preparation for him to learn the rules. Make sure to play along and yawn and even snore.

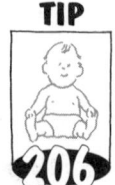

Reward the child in the big bed

Put your child to sleep in her own bed, and reward her by saying, "Now that you are a big girl, you can go to bed at 8:15." (Maybe bedtime was 8:00 before this.) Remain with her for a few minutes, but gradually move farther away from her bed. One mom likes to sit at the foot of the bed so it's easier to make it out the door. It may take a few days, but soon she should learn to go to sleep in her own room.

"Say goodnight to everyone who loves you"

Now that he is a little older, have him say goodnight to all the people who love him. Make the list really long (you can include his nursery school teacher and other kids in his class) and try shutting your eyes and whispering throughout this ritual.

Go on monster patrol

Sprinkle fairy dust to ward off monsters. Let your child help sprinkle the dust—just make sure you don't use talc; it's not safe to inhale. Consider going on monster patrol to show the child that the monster-hiding places are empty. Put up a sign: "NO MONSTERS ALLOWED IN THIS ROOM." In other words, *take this seriously* because it is serious to your child. When my daughter was little, I would call over the intercom to the doorman to see if they "let monsters in." I would ask: "Henry, do you let monsters in to this building?" And Henry would respond, "Absolutely not, madam." In the morning, the doorman would wink at my daughter and say, "No monsters, right?"

Read <u>The Tooth Fairies' Nighttime Visit</u>

This is a good book for ages three and up. As an added bonus, the book, *The Tooth Fairies' Nighttime Visit*, by Cecile Schoberle (Simon & Schuster, 1999), has 36 glitter stickers. "Bedtime's here, so turn off the light, It's time for the tooth fairies' wondrous flight." The book shows the tooth fairies looking for sleeping children and leaving special treats.

TIP

Say prayers

As part of your nightly ritual of saying goodnight to people and things your child loves, you might also add a little prayer for each. This is particularly valid if you personally think that there IS someone up there listening. You can start with your own prayers and let your child bless who they want to—his list may change over time.

Read <u>Good Night, God Bless</u>

A lovely book for "teaching" prayers is *Good Night, God Bless* by Susan Heyboer O'Keefe, illustrated by Hideko Takahashi (Henry Holt & Co., 1999). At the close of the day, the air cools, lights dim, and animals big and small settle down to sleep. Inside houses, children perform nighttime rituals before snuggling up in bed to say their prayers. This book puts an emphasis on good old-fashioned security of home and family; the child moves through familiar places and faces and blesses each one for another day. ("Good night, God bless, All creatures; sleep, The air now hushed of growl and peep.")

Special reward

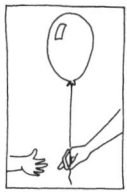

Put a special reward under your toddler's pillow, for her to discover in the morning. This is a variation on the tooth fairy job—you are now also the gift fairy who leaves a small reward on the pillow on the occasion of a good night's sleep. This makes waking up more pleasurable and reinforces sleeping through the night without wake-ups.

TIP

Limit liquids at bedtime

Be careful of what you give your child before bedtime. Limit liquids to maybe just a small cup of water. In general, give only lukewarm liquids after dinner. Cold stimulates and also can cause tummy aches. Similarly avoid cold snacks near bedtime, because it can stimulate the child while delaying digestion and making it harder to fall asleep.

Parent-to-parent: Give warm milk

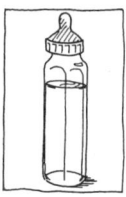

"I was taught that once they begin to drink their milk or formula cold, if you give them only cold bottles during the day and then warm the last one before bedtime, it has a calming effect on the child."

In this case, I am talking about a toddler who can have a little warm milk before bed. I recommend you give a little warm water as the last few sips. This is to satisfy all those dentists out there who are concerned that anything left in the mouth other than water could increase the chance of developing cavities.

Turn over an hourglass

As the sands of time trickle down, you can tell your child she will also trickle off into sleep. Just watching the sand pour through is hypnotic and peaceful. The story of the sandman is an Arabian myth your child might enjoy.

Waking up from napping

After their first birthday, most children resent being woken up from a nap. So let him take frequent catnaps if he seems to prefer that, or live with the long midday crash nap that other toddlers require. The more you cater to a child's sleep needs during the day, the less difficult the night sleep will be.

Forget logic: Very tired toddlers have trouble sleeping

Sometimes logic doesn't work. Common sense might tell you if you tire your toddler out, she will sleep longer. Often the opposite is true. The paradox is that if she is too excited and overtired, she has more trouble calming down and going to sleep.

TIP

Let's hear it for night-lights

For a while, night-lights fell out of favor. They come in a great variety of sizes and shapes. (Disney characters are always very popular.) The best kinds have low-wattage electric bulbs that don't flicker or throw scary shadows. They often help to calm a child if she wakes up in the middle of the night. Some children should also have a light they can turn on at will. Don't use one of those light-sensitive night-lights—just opening and closing a door can cause it to go on and off and that can be scary. (Also make sure the pathway to the bathroom is lit.)

Brrr!

A child may wake up if he is cold. Toddlers are natural tossers, turners, and kickers; they get tangled up in their blankets, and then kick them off. Consider putting your child in a cozy blanket sleeper or specially designed sleeping bag for warmth

Toddler sleep review

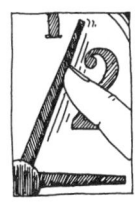

Between the second and third birthdays, toddlers need about 11 hours of sleep a night and a single hour-and-a-half nap during the day. Most children this age go to bed sometime between 7 and 9 P.M. and get up between 6:30 and 8 A.M. While it may seem that your child's sleeping habits finally are more like yours, he will spend more time in light REM sleep until about 4 A.M., when he might briefly get up to pee. What that means is he makes more transitions from one sleep phase to the next and will wake up more often. He needs to have learned how to soothe himself right back to sleep.

"One more, no more"

Change the bedtime routine a little to accommodate the fact that your toddler may have a lot of requests. At the toddler stage, she will ask for just one more story, one more glass of water, one last kiss. Anticipate this by adding another story, getting her water—just make sure there is a limit. You can repeat the line, "One more, no more," until she learns to say it: "Okay Daddy, I know, one more, no more." Some of the cleverest stalling techniques have been thought up by toddlers at this witching hour. One of my favorites is a three-year-old who said she forgot to do something really, really important, and then ran out to say, "sleep tight, good night" for the sixth time—to the television set.

Nighttime concerns

Toddlers (and preschoolers) have more nighttime worries. They still need to check for monsters. Suddenly they are afraid of the dark or loud noises, and they may need to be comforted and reassured. This is a good time to incorporate stories at bedtime that relate to what your child experienced during the day. If he had a weird day in the sandbox, you might say, "Boy we had a rough day at the playground, didn't we? That kid really wanted your ball, didn't he? But didn't we have fun when we went to the duck pond?" Don't worry that you could be inducing nightmares. Far from it. Talking about problem spots before sleep helps diffuse the incident. But if you say *nothing*, you might hear your child moaning in his sleep and actually hear the word, "ball."

Just say no...to sedatives

No matter how much trouble you have with your child and sleep, do not even think of giving your child a sedative before bedtime. They are difficult to dose and the side effects include restlessness and confusion. They can even cause nightmares. Similarly, don't give any version of an adult cough or cold medicine. Adult Nyquil, for example, is loaded with alcohol, which has been known to cause immediate agitation followed by stuporous, unnatural sleep. Don't do it!

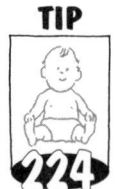

Concept of time

Understand that children have a limited understanding of the concept of time. So give specific warnings: "Bedtime will be in ten minutes; put your toys away right now." He doesn't *really* know what "ten minutes" is, but you can show him on the clock, and then remind him when the ten minutes are up. (Reassure him that his toys, stuffed animals, and building blocks will still be there for him in the morning.) Use a ticking timer to illustrate time passing.

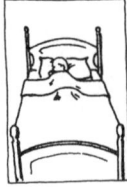

Adult beds are for adults

Sleeping alone is a learned developmental step. I'm not even sure if it's "natural," but most of us prefer it over the family bed in this culture. This is another reason why your adult bed should be off-limits to children in the evenings. A young child generally sleeps better alone. He shouldn't have to depend on the security of your bed to be able to feel safe.

Restless sleepers, part I

What do you do if your little ones get restless during the night? Safety considerations have to come first. Make sure there is no access to the kitchen, garage, staircases, or any other potentially dangerous place. Do whatever it takes. If your child is not yet toilet trained, then make sure she can't get into the bathroom, which can be full of dangers to a little one—put an external latch high up on the door.

TIP

Restless sleepers, part II

Sometimes for restless sleepers, you can cut back on daytime naps or make bedtime a little later. It sounds good on paper, but it isn't foolproof. But you might as well try it, you never know. Restless sleepers may also need a change in daytime scheduling to avoid getting overtired. Always consider other potential factors like his diet or his television exposure.

Keep to your ritual wherever you are

Stick to your bedtime routines wherever you are. If you are at Aunt Sophie's house or at a hotel, still sing the same lullaby, etcetera, and stick to the routine as closely as possible. Bring whatever pieces of the ritual can be easily carried—like a favorite pillow, blanky, and book. Then add a new, special piece to the bedtime ritual just for the trip. When you get home, you can say, "Let's do that Holiday Inn bedtime thing we did."

Waking from napping, revisited

Although the rule is to let sleeping children sleep, you may have to wake a toddler from her nap if it is too long. For example, if she nods off at 11:30 A.M. and now it's 3 P.M., then she has missed at least one meal and will not be ready to go to bed for several hours. Understand, she will not be thrilled to be woken. Don't rush her up. Unless you have to get her up, let the transition last for a while. Touch her gently, uncover her, turn on the lights, put on Raffi. Then come back in five minutes. She may be awake on her own.

Reschedule naps

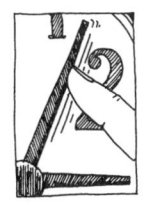

As we've seen, naps get cut back to about once a day just before her second birthday. If she has given up her morning nap, she will get cranky at the usual naptime. You may have to rethink your decision to sign up for "Mom and Me" swim class if it's scheduled at her usual naptime. Give her a chance to have some quiet time, about 20 minutes, in place of her nap. It might help to give her an earlier afternoon nap so she can have lunch and then nap. She will still have plenty of time for dinner and evening activities before bed.

Counting sheep

Although counting sheep is popularly touted as the way to get adults to go to sleep, it's not so reliable for children. But if your child is learning to count, you might try counting something fun. I liked to make up a story of how it came to be that counting sheep put people to sleep. As I see it, there was a family of shepherds. Dad said to his son, Enoch, "Before you go to bed, go out to the pasture and count the sheep." Enoch would go out and get so bored counting the flock, he would fall fast asleep. And his dad would say, "Enoch, you did it again, you fell asleep counting the sheep." (Feel free to come up with your own explanation!)

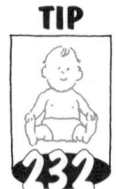

The roaming toddler

If a toddler roams at night, *do not* lock the bedroom door, or stretch netting over his crib, or put him in any kind of sleep harness. It's dangerous and makes sleeping equal to prison. It is a terrible thing for a child to be banging on the door or trying to be a miniature Houdini breaking out of restraints. If you are determined to stop your wanderer in his tracks (and not have to keep returning him to his room), it's far better to put up a gate across his door. And don't forget to be particularly careful if there are stairs. Put a gate in front of the staircase and a bell on his door. Make sure your toddler can't knock over gates or simply leap over them. (Another rather sweet product I picked up at a convention recently is a gate made by Childcraft. It beeps loudly if security has been breached.)

The bedroom

The toddler's bedroom should be a place where nice things happen. The child's bed should be special, with bedding she has chosen. The child should start to develop a sense of ownership. This is her space. The bedroom might have a table with picture books, a child-friendly tape recorder, and a lamp with a 15-watt lightbulb. As much as possible, let your toddler help pick out what goes into her room—certainly she should have a choice of picture books.

FYI: General sleep fact

Think of sleep as energy that recharges the brain's battery. It's been observed that sleeping well increases brainpower, almost like Wonder bread builds strong bones. Sleep has even been known to cure some ailments. When we sleep, the body actually makes more antibodies and white blood cells, which form the body's army of defense against infection. One of the reasons we sleep more when we are sick is a chemical cascade that seems to be saying, "OK, we need to make more antibodies and white cells, put this body to sleep for a while." When a child sleeps well, he is also more likely to wake well. If a child doesn't sleep well, he is more likely to stay drowsy or be cranky all day.

When parents' bedtime styles clash

Sometimes parents have markedly different bedtime styles. I suggest you divide up the bedtime chores and have a calendar that shows who is "on." It's very important that you don't play good cop, bad cop when it comes to sleep. If you do, then your child will naturally go to the "good" sleep cop to get what he wants. Rather, choose different nights for each parent. One parent may even learn from the other. And never, ever argue about bedtime in front of the other parent. I suggest the parent who is not on call use this time to take a bath or even go out for a walk, as soon as your child is comfortable with this system.

"There never was a child so lovely"

"There never was a child so lovely but his Mother was glad to see him asleep."

—Ralph Waldo Emerson

Translation: You can really, really love your child and still put him to bed. I love this quote quite a lot. You are also in good company if you sometimes think you love your child the most when he *is* asleep.

Sing "Lullaby and Good Night" ("Brahms' Lullaby")

This is truly an oldie but a goody. It still works!

Lullaby, and good night,
With pink roses bedtight,
With lilies o'erspread
Is my baby's sweet head.
Let you down now, and rest,
May your slumber be blessed!
Lay you down now, and rest,
May thy slumber be blessed!

Lullaby, and good night,
You're your mother's delight,
Shining angels beside
My darling abide.
Soft and warm is your bed,
Close your eyes and rest your head.
Sleepyhead, close your eyes.
Mother's right here beside you.

I'll protect you from harm,
You will wake in my arms.
Guardian angels are near,
So sleep on, with no fear.
Guardian angels are near,
So sleep on, with no fear.

Sleep log

If child has sleep problems, or you just think she does, consider keeping a sleep log or diary. It's just a tool to see how your child is sleeping and what routinely keeps her up. It's also a good idea to look and see what her daytime schedule is like as well.

Sample sleep log:

<u>Event</u>	<u>Time</u>	<u>"Quality"</u>
Woke up	7 A.M.	grouchy
A.M. nap	10 A.M.–noon	sound asleep
P.M. nap	2–3 P.M.	restless
Bedtime	8 P.M.	trouble settling down
Woke up crying	1 A.M.	put herself back to sleep
Nightmares	2 A.M.	needed 5 min rule for 20 min

12-36 MONTHS: TODDLERS

Waking a child at naptime

When your toddler starts taking long naps late in the day, it's not likely he'll easily go to sleep at a reasonable time. You need to gently rouse your toddler an hour or so into the nap. Toddlers can be very unpleasant and even violent when they are woken up—much like certain teenagers I know. If your child thrashes and kicks when you come near, let well-chosen music and cool air do the job—remotely—instead.

TIP

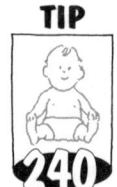

Establish an earlier bedtime

Worth repeating: Parents are afraid of establishing an earlier bedtime because they think that will cause the child to get up earlier. Actually, the opposite is true. And so is the converse: Too late a bedtime will cause a child to wake too early. Sleep causes sleep. All of this may not seem entirely logical, but it is biological.

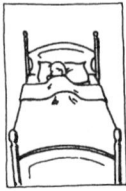

Wake-up time

Parents always talk a lot about bedtime, but what about wake-up time? Should parents act as alarm clocks? One school advises yes; if a child goes to bed between 6 and 8 P.M., her parents should wake her between 6 and 7 A.M. I say, once again, wake a child in the morning only if you have to—maybe you have a doctor's appointment. Otherwise, heavens no.

Disturbances

Thunderstorms, darkness, dogs, trucks, and even clowns can easily disturb the two- to four-year-old. If you can name it, some toddler is afraid of it. Such fears are usually short lived, and the scary things come and go. ("Gee Mom, this year can I have a clown at my birthday party?") Often the child can be cured by reassurance, open doors, night-lights. Make sure your child has his own flashlight that he can turn on at will. This is another opportunity to remind you to be careful what the child sees and hears during the day. Unmonitored television can be a source of great anxiety—it's hard for children to interpret the often disturbing images on the news. Actually, it's pretty upsetting for adults as well.

Yoga breathing

If your child has trouble going to sleep, or wakes up during the night, there are some breathing exercises you can do with her. Yoga breathing is particularly helpful. Make sure your child is in bed and the lights are out. Tell her: "Take a big breath in—and push your belly out; now breathe all the way out and watch your belly shrink." If concentrating on "belly out and belly down" is too complicated, then just let her take deep, slow breaths in and out through her nose. (Steam her first if she has a cold.)

These exercises not only relax the mind and body but also are wonderful for children with asthma.

"Relax your toes"

Here's another relaxation technique that works with children of all ages. Again, the child should be in bed, with the lights out. Have the child tighten and then relax various body parts. You can start at the bottom—"relax your toes"—and work your way up, or you can mix body parts—"relax your toes and your hands." Don't forget to have her open her mouth wide and stretch and then relax. This is known as sequential relaxation and is often used in stress reduction therapies of many kinds. (I thank my chiropractor for this one.)

Prerecord bedtime stores

If one parent is frequently not home at bedtime or travels often, have that parent tape-record one or two of the child's favorite stories. The absent parent can still be there at bedtime. Most children love having their very own CD or tape so they can control the "coming and going" of the person on it.

Obstructive sleep apnea (OSA)

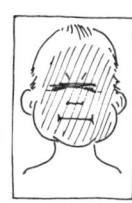

OSA is characterized by loud snoring and disrupted sleep. It is caused mainly by enlarged tonsils and/or adenoids blocking the upper airway during sleep. The result is a reduction in necessary oxygen getting to the child's organs. OSA is treated in extreme cases by surgically removing the tonsils and/or adenoids. In milder cases, you can treat the child the same way you would if she had a stuffed nose using warm steam and saline nose drops. If you are not sure exactly what you are dealing with, videotape your sleeping child and show the tape to your pediatrician. A picture, with sound, is truly worth a thousand words. These children often have daytime irritability and if previously toilet trained, may experience accidents.

Read *Sleep, Little One, Sleep*

Here's a charming book, *Sleep, Little One, Sleep*, by Marion Dane Bauer (Simon & Schuster, 1999), about a father reading to his child. As the sun sets, the father puts his child to bed, weaving images of mice, birds, and polar bears. He tells her: "Sleep nibbles the last crumbs of day; . . . Sleep holds her tight in the dark." By the last page, Dad is nodding off, and the child is dreaming of flying on a polar bear. (Recommended for ages one to four.)

Toddlers and traveling

Another word about jet lag: If possible, toddlers should fly during the day. Being on the plane is stimulating, so chances are your toddler won't sleep during the trip. Let her run up and down the aisles! Ideally, on arrival it will be bedtime, and your toddler will be tired.

Rituals for wake-up

Create some pleasant wake-up rituals, which could include your own personalized good-morning song.

Here's one a parent sang every morning until her son reached the age of three.

"Good morning, Mr. Scott, Good morning, Mr. Scott.

Just so you know it, we love you a lot.

Good morning, Mr. Scott, Good morning, Mr. Scott.

Let's check your diaper and see what we got."

TIP

Wake-up cuddles

When your toddler wakes up in the morning, encourage her to cuddle with you.

Actually, when *any* age child wakes up she should cuddle with you. That sets the tone for the day, which spills (we hope) over into the next night. Close physical contact is the stuff good dreams and happy thoughts are made of. Don't be caught short when next asked, "Have you hugged your child today?"

TIP

Family bed: Good morning, world

Here's my personally modified version of the family bed. In the morning, I would play an old '50s song, "Bop." As soon as my children heard the distinctive intro beat, they knew that was the signal to come in and jump into bed. Then we would all sing. We would get really comfy. This was a fun activity that helped the entire family wake up and enjoy the coming day.

Cold medicine

I strongly recommend that you try out cold medicines on your toddler during the day—not at night. Dose lightly at first to test for undesired side effects. I recently got a frantic call in the middle of the night from a parent whose child is always sensitive to medicine. The parent decided the child needed cold medicine to go to sleep, but instead her child was up all night staring and saying, "Mommy, I'm scared."

Croup: The illness

Croup is a viral illness that causes a narrowing of the upper airway. This is a scary condition with its own set of unique symptoms. It occurs suddenly and almost always in the night. It routinely dissipates by the morning, only to return again the next night. It usually affects children between the ages of one and three. It's hard to miss because it sounds as if your child has transformed into a barking seal. If there is any doubt, call the pediatrician—yes, even if it's the middle of the night—and let her listen. It generally lasts for three nights. Forget sleeping alone that night, but try to appear calm, soothing, and in control. When your child is croupy, all sleeping bets are off—this is not the time to worry about sleep training.

Croup: The treatment

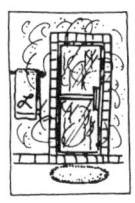

Never give cold medicines to a child with croup. During the day, after the first night of croup, you can help prepare your child's airway so she can sleep better at night. I strongly recommend steaming frequently. As often as five minutes every hour, especially as it gets later in the day. You want to humidify the throat. (Steaming revisited: Turn shower on full blast hot and close the bathroom door for 15 minutes to build up the steam. Close the shower door or curtain before entering the bathroom [not the shower] with the child. Hold child in your arms to avoid risking contact with hot water.)

TIP

Final words on croup

If your child has difficulty breathing, don't make her lie down flat at night. Not only will she just pop right back up, but sitting up and leaning forward makes it easier for her to breathe. But keep the lights off. You want to keep her calm so her airways won't swell, but she still needs to know that it's nighttime.

Earaches

Having an earache is a common reason why children get up; it often gets worse at night. The child should be slightly elevated, because the fluid drains away when he is sitting up. You can relieve some of the symptoms by using any warmed oil—and I really mean *any*. It could be mineral oil, olive oil, vegetable oil, or even baby oil. Either use a dropper or soak a cotton ball and insert into the ear canal. *Never* use oil for a child who has any kind of ear discharge or has had tubes surgically placed in his ears.

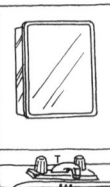

The medicine cabinet for toddlers

Here are some suggestions of items to keep in your medicine cabinet.

- thermometer
- antihistamine and decongestant (if agitated, then just antihistamine)
- chamomile tea
- age-appropriate cold medicine
- age-appropriate antacid
- children's Tylenol and Motrin (or generic equivalents)

Sunburn

If your toddler has sunburn that interferes with his sleep, give him an antihistamine. Give diphenhydramine (Benadryl) and Motrin for pain one hour before bedtime. (It takes about an hour for the swelling to go down.) You might offer the child a tepid bath and a mentholated topical gel like Rhuli gel. And then put him to sleep in a slightly warm room.

Note: You should try to avoid your child getting sunburned in the first place. Sunburn is not only likely to ruin any chance of a good night's sleep, it is also dangerous to your child's health—present and future. Sunburn in infancy can be the prelude to getting skin cancers later on. Check out netting systems that can be zipped over a stroller or carriage. A recently introduced system has specially treated netting that adds UVS and UVB sun protection, just perfect for midday strolling.

Painkillers

For pain, give toddlers Tylenol or Motrin/Advil. (*Note:* Motrin and Advil are ibuprofen. No brand product endorsement is intended.) Is your child a "drinker" or a "chewer"? In other words, at night is he more likely to want to drink or chew his medicine? If you have a choice, use a liquid form of medicine because chewing can stimulate a child. Some kids however, will not take any medicine by mouth. Tylenol is available in a suppository form. Try these remedies out in the daytime to discover which of the myriad flavor choices your child most easily accepts. Nighttime is not the time to be conducting a survey.

Insect bites

Use an anesthetic spray for insect bites. Again Rhuligel or Rhulispray is soothing. Aveeno makes a soothing powder that can be added to the bath. Your child will come out looking a lot like an oatmeal ghoul, but she will feel cool and comfortable. You can also try an over-the-counter hydrocortisone steroid cream, but avoid eyes and mouth.

Gas

If your toddler has gas, you can use the child version of many adult treatments for gas. Try Tums or children's Mylanta or calcium carbonate, which is available in both a liquid and chewable form. For calming, try a hot water bottle, but be careful to cover and seal it tightly. (And don't forget chamomile tea.)

"A spoonful of sugar"

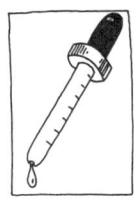

Many medicines just taste nasty. There is nothing worse than trying to force-feed bad-tasting medicine to a sick child in the middle of the night. All you will get is a screaming child who may even throw up. Try to make the experience as pleasant as possible. You want to get the medicine down, and then get out of the room. It's become more common for pharmacies to add flavor to some medicines. In some cases they add medicines *to* the flavors. In New York City, Bigelow Pharmacy will add just about any medicine to any flavor. A pharmacist in Washington, D.C., has a recipe book that lists 42 different flavors to be mixed into most children's medicines. Your pharmacy or doctor can call 1-800-884-5771 if they are not familiar with FLAVORx. You could buy a special pacifier that comes with a little attached reservoir meant for giving medicine. This works for babies who still suck on pacifiers.

Vomiting

Vomiting at night is a common ploy of toddlers. It can be intentional or gastronomical. Either way, if you know your child screams for attention and then vomits, don't go with your first instinct, which may be to do just about anything to stop it from happening. Don't run in at the first scream or you will teach your child to scream. Just quickly clean up in the dark with little reaction. (Obviously, if child is vomiting because he's sick, then you treat it as you would any illness.)

Pillows, revisited

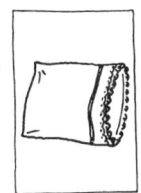

I am often asked at what age a child can officially have a pillow. Generally, babies can safely have a pillow at age two. But understand that children younger than that often create pillows by putting a stuffed animal under their head. If your child does that, then go in quietly and move it from under his head. You can leave it against his body for comfort. If you are using a pillow to elevate your child due to congestion, then make sure it is hard and stiff, so he can't sink into it. (Even if your child is not allergic, I recommend avoiding down pillows. If your child is congested, he can inhale feather particles, which may magnify the congestion.)

Just say no...to television

Don't get into the habit of letting your child watch television late into the night when she is sick. That could just create sleep problems later on. Sometimes adults turn on the television because they are bored and don't know how to stay up late without it or because the child begs for TV. Set limits: TV is off-limits. Otherwise, your child will demand television when she is well. Television viewing is practically an Olympic event in the United States. The average school-age child watches four hours a day. No wonder we are the fattest nation on earth.

The sleeping bag solution

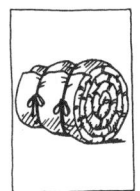

Here's a trick some kids consider a real treat. It's good for the child who has trouble going back to her own bed, for whatever the reason. Let your child sleep in a sleeping bag in your room. Every day move the sleeping bag farther and farther away from the bed. Make a map and mark on a calendar the path the sleeping bag is taking. At the end of the week, or whatever time period you note on the calendar, the child should find a treasure waiting in her room—where her sleeping bag is now situated.

Bedtime snacks

A bedtime snack should contain foods high in tryptophan, a natural amino acid thought to help induce sleep when it is converted into serotonin. Turkey is one food loaded with tryptophan, but I have a problem imagining children gobbling up turkey before bedtime. Consider giving other healthy foods like fruit and whole grains, soft cheese and crackers, or yogurt.

Decongest your house

Particles in the air may contribute to nasal stuffiness and irritated eyes, which can easily awaken a sleeping child. Even if your child isn't known to have allergies per se, the house should be a "no smoking" area. Also avoid perfume, hair spray, and paint fumes, which can all be irritants. Wash your child's clothes and bedclothes before using, and keep the dust bunnies at bay.

TIP 269

Sing a Welsh lullaby

If you are good with accents, this one could be fun for both of you. I sang it with an Irish brogue, which was about as close as I could get, but it worked.

A mother was pressing her babe to her breast
And saying while soothing his sorrow to rest
Sleep gently my darling, sleep soundly my boy
For thou art my treasure, my rapture and joy
The trumpet is howling again and again
Thy father is sailing a-far on the main
May heav'n be his shield on the deep heaving sea
And bring him in safety to thee and to me

The lightning was vivid, the thunder was loud
The mother was praying, and sobbing aloud
Amid the wild moaning of nature in strife
The captain sprang forward, and flew to his wife
He kiss'd the fond mother, he kiss'd his dear boy
And gazed on them kindly, exclaiming with joy
"I've made a good fortune, and never will roam
Again from my wife, my sweet child, and my home."

Sing an Irish lullaby ("Too-Ra-Loo-Ra-Loo")

This was a favorite of Yvonne, my son David's first nanny. I can still hear her lulling us both to sleep.

Over in Killarney
Many years ago,
Me mither sang a song to me
In tones so sweet and low.

Just a simple little ditty,
In her good ould Irish way,
And I'd give the world if she could sing
That song to me this day.

Too-ra-loo-ra-loo-ral,
Too-ra-loo-ra-li
Too-ra-loo-ra-loo-ral
Hush, now don't you cry

Too-ra-loo-ra-loo-ral,
Too-ra-loo-ra-li,
Too-ra-loo-ra-loo-ral,
That's an Irish lullaby.

12-36 MONTHS: TODDLERS

Nighttime walks

Make an effort to go out for a walk just before bed every night with your child. Many of my parents regularly go out before they wind down for the night. The brief period of exercise and fresh air seems to help the child prepare for sleep. Make it a stroll, not a power walk, of course.

Read <u>Good Night, Gorilla</u>

Toddlers love to follow the antics of the gorilla in *Good Night, Gorilla* by Peggy Rathman (G. Putnam's Sons, 1994) as he lets all of the animals out of the zoo and then brings them back. This version is also a good size for little hands.

Set up an aquarium

There's a reason why many dentists have aquariums in their office. Aquariums are hypnotic and actually calm patients. In your child's room, an aquarium can also act as a night-light. The water, the fish, the sounds of the filter all help to lull a child to sleep. And it also counts as a pet.

Nightmares

Children are susceptible to scary dreams and are easily disturbed by them. When you go in to comfort your child, don't just say "go back to sleep." Do not raise your voice. Keep her company; sit on the bed. Listen. The idea is to let her put the dream in perspective. Take it seriously, and don't counter with logic. In other words, it won't help to point out that unicorns don't exist!

Calming nightmares

You may want to change the atmosphere. Put on a night-light or a soft light. Play soft music. The idea is for the child to see you are in control of the environment. But the child should remain in, or be returned to, her bed. You want the child to feel that her room is not scary.

Really listen to what seems to be upsetting your child. One of my parents told me her seven-year-old was having nightmares after the death of her grandfather and was getting up in the middle of the night and putting on a light. I suggested that for the next few nights, the light be *left on* for the child. This really helped her a lot through this tough period.

Nightmare prevention

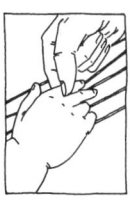

Sometimes you can stop a nightmare in its tracks or prevent one from happening. This depends on the power of suggestion. I believed in telling my children that they had the power to stop their nightmares. My daughter believed that if she could just squeeze her pillow hard, she would immediately wake up and the nightmare would end. To this day, it works.

Some people believe that there are trigger points on the hands that can prevent bad dreams. (Have your child press her index finger down as far as it goes onto her palm. Presto! Now she will have good dreams.)

Night terrors

In night terrors, the child cries *during* the episode. Unlike nightmares, they occur *earlier* on in sleep. This is a neurological event related to the immature nervous system of children about one to three years old. (The brain can send electrical signals that are received as startling images.) Your child may not have any idea why she is scared, and often she cannot recall the dream in the morning. When you go in to comfort her, she may seem to be disoriented and sweating. Don't panic if she doesn't make sense and is muttering about snakes or monsters. Help your child to gradually return to reality. Keep her company until the episode has played itself out. Don't shake her awake or even try to wake her. You may still be upset while she just goes back to sleep.

If this happens very often, you should report this to your pediatrician. Night terrors can be a predictor that your child may be a future sleepwalker as well.

Peeking in on your toddler

Parents often get nervous at night and want to check up on their toddler. Maybe the child went to bed with a cold or a fever. Typically, if a parent peeks in, the toddler catches them and wakes right up. Here's a great, sort of sneaky way to avoid being caught in the act. Position a mirror or glass-framed picture on a wall to help you peek into the room without having to open the door all the way. (*Tip:* If you do open the door a little, make sure you regularly oil the hinges so the door won't creak and give you away.) Another trick that worked with my son was for me to lie on my belly and peek around the door. He wasn't expecting me at "commando level" and was focusing higher up where he expected me to appear.

In some cultures babies <u>are</u> given alcohol

There are those cultures where wine and sometimes beer—in the form of lager or heavy malt—are given routinely right along with milk. My advice is don't beat yourself up if once in a great while your child falls off the wagon, so to speak. Many years ago, when my son David was two, my husband and I decided to go out to a French restaurant for a romantic dinner. We sat at a table with candles. David sat in his stroller beside us—the babysitter didn't show up—and cried. The very French waiter simply whisked away David's bottle and disappeared into the kitchen. When he returned, the bottle had a distinctly grapish tint. David sucked it right down and slept soundly throughout the meal. As far as I can tell, he was no worse for the experience and we enjoyed an uninterrupted meal.

3-6 Years: Preschoolers

Reinforce bedtime

Different generations had different styles. Our parents simply kissed us, tucked us in, and turned out the lights. This routine didn't account for the fact that children don't just turn off like the light. (That is why so many of us recall sneaking out and eavesdropping on adult conversations.) Once children are capable of opening the door, we have to help them wind down and stay down. Understand that you can't will a preschooler to go to sleep. Children go to sleep when they are tired, not necessarily when *you* are tired. Let your children know what time they are expected to be in bed. (Be specific: "When the big hand is on the…") Go through any bedtime routines you have established, and then shut the door or close it most of the way. (Leave a night-light on if necessary.) You are reinforcing the notion that the child has her own responsibilities and that it is a good thing to have a bedtime.

Set limits

You can't command sleep, but you do have a right to set behavioral limits. For instance, you can say, "No, you can't come out of your room. I want you to stay in bed until morning. You can read with a light on, but the rest of the house is off-limits." Be *specific* about the quiet activities your child can do while in bed. He can read or he can listen to soft music. You can get a wandering child to wander back to his bedroom by making sure being out of his room isn't pleasurable. Don't offer any extras to coax him back in—no juice, or kisses, or stories. Just repeat, "It's time for bed now." And do not debate the issue.

Read <u>Can't You Sleep, Little Bear?</u> to dispel fear of the dark

Read *Can't You Sleep, Little Bear?*, by Martin Waddell (Candlewick Press, 1988), to help your child get rid of his fear of the dark. This book, for ages three and up, is a look at a small bear's fear of the dark and how the big bear parent reassures the baby bear.

Read Goodnight (A Pop-up Lullaby) just for the giggles

Read this book, *Goodnight (A Pop-up Lullaby)* by Jan Pienkowski (Candlewick Press, 1999), for giggles before bedtime. It's time for bed. "But wait there's a skunk in my bunk. There are ants in my pants. There's a gnu in my shoe." This book provides a list of whimsical (and rhyming) reasons why a child tries to postpone bedtime.

The early riser

You can teach a very early riser to look at a clock and see, for example, that when the number is 7, it means it's OK to get Mommy or Daddy. Some parents have learned the hard way to put an index card over the last numbers of a digital clock—otherwise the child may come out when it's 4:27. With digital clocks all the rage, some children rarely have the opportunity to learn how to tell time from a "real" clock. Find a fun clock—maybe one that has a face on it, and its eyes close when it snoozes. Then you can tell your child, "See, the clock is sleeping, too."

Make a dream catcher

During the day, create a Native American dream catcher with your preschooler. Dream catchers are supposed to trap the bad dreams while allowing the good dreams to slide down and into her mind. (Of course, you can purchase one from a Native American crafts catalogue.)

TIP

Prebedtime rules

Don't just set bedtime rules, also set up rules for what he can do *before* he goes to sleep. He can't just go from playing to "Okay, you're done for the day now it's time for sleep." Help him change gears by announcing, "Okay, in ten minutes we will put away all our electric gizmos…" The idea is to gradually decrease all stimulation—all those fun things like watching television and playing video games. Aim for the wind down to begin at least ten minutes before you expect to start the bedtime ritual.

Make sleep a priority "chore," not a punishment

Sleep has to be a priority right along with brushing his teeth and cleanup.

One way to do this is to make sure that going to bed is always put in a positive light. Going to sleep should never be used as a punishment. Send him to his room but not to his bed. Never threaten, "You were bad today so you have to go to bed an hour early." Tell your child regularly how wonderful sleep is—have a pajama party to celebrate the wonderfulness of sleep.

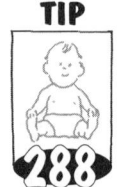

Parent-to-parent: Read <u>In the Night Kitchen</u>

"I must have read this book five thousand times to put Carmello and Emilio to sleep, from the time they were nine months all the way up to four. I never remembered the exact title. We always referred to it as the 'Milk in the Batter' book, because that is one of the jingles in the middle of the book. It's part of: 'Stir it, Scrape it! Make it, Bake it!' Check it out for yourself." (*In the Night Kitchen,* by Maurice Sendak, Harper & Row, 1970.)

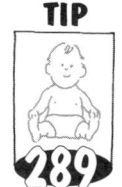

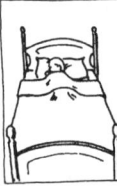

Napping

Napping doesn't affect sleep in the preschooler. Four-year-olds who nap or sleep the *same* number of hours as children who don't nap. And they don't make up for a missed nap by sleeping more, so sleep "missed" is never made up. You may put your child down to rest because *you* need a break.

However, do not allow an older child to nap through *most* of the afternoon if you expect to sleep at night at her regular time. If your four-year-old is exhausted after preschool, an hour nap when she gets home should be enough. Help her wake up by pulling back the blanket and turning on the lights.

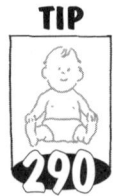

Recommended daily sleep allowance

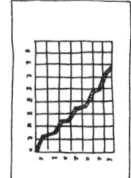

By four, the average amount of sleep is down to about 12 hours, which includes napping. The older child who still naps is likely to get up early or stay up late. Some even require as little as ten hours. (They often sleep more when they experience a growth spurt.) Remember of course that sleep needs vary from child to child and stage to stage—allow for variations within reason.

Connection between sleep and illness

If your child sleeps an extraordinary amount, for him, don't even think of sending him off to preschool the next day. There's a good chance the sleep was caused by the body's fighting off illness. Often a parent will tell me that their child came home from school and slept straight through until the parent woke the child the next morning. Then the child is sent off to school only to be sent home with a high fever. (I have seen this scenario played out over and over because parents don't make the connection between oversleeping and being sick.) I also believe in occasional "personal" days when even a preschooler is allowed to sleep in.

Create a tent

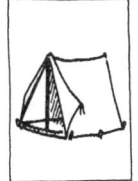

Make a safety tent with your child. Most children love the adventure of sleeping in a tent, even if the tent is just on their bed. You can make a tent out of her bedding. Just use lightweight material that breathes—you don't want your child to be cooking inside the tent. Childhood should always be fun, and camping in is fun.

3-6 YEARS: PRESCHOOLERS

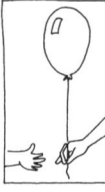

Reward cooperation

If your preschooler gets up at night and you carry or put him back to bed without a fuss, then in the morning praise him for cooperating with you. Maybe give him a small reward. You can also reward a child for a partial success—even though he got out of bed, he did go back to bed and stay there. (I like to stress that a partial success should not be viewed as a failure.) Just make sure the child knows you are rewarding him for going back to sleep, and not for getting out of bed in the first place. Of course, praise the child who does stay in bed all night all the more.

Make a bedtime star chart

Create a bedtime star chart for your preschooler. To make sure he knows the rules, read them to him: "Stay in bed, read, be quiet, go to sleep, stay in bed all night." Give stars when he complies, and let a certain number of stars equal a predetermined reward or a surprise one for kids who love suspense. Some parents hang the chart right on the bedroom door as a reminder.

Connect the reward to bedtime

Children love new things—from toys to books. You can reward a child with just about anything, but I like the idea of it being connected to sleep as reinforcement. It would be a nice idea to let your child choose a new pair of pajamas or maybe a pair of oversized doggy slippers. Let picking out the gift be part of the process. (Chances are you will have a happy little superhero or heroine leaping off to bed.) In general, your preschooler should be making a variety of independent decisions connected to sleep every day. Picking out the bedtime story or choosing a song to sing are some examples.

The 20-minute solution

Add more time for your child to fall asleep when he is a preschooler. It takes an average of an extra 20 minutes to go to sleep at naptime and up to an hour at bedtime to make the transition to sleep. Again, give your child a warning as you go from one transition to another. Even if he doesn't officially fall asleep at naptime, if he has 20 minutes of quiet time, it counts. Studies indicate that 20 minutes of quiet time is as good as two hours of sleep. Resting the mind brings rest to the entire body. At this age, children can "shut off" the brain during rest. Most adults can't will their brains to shut down.

Sleepwalking

Sleepwalking is inherited by 10 to 15 percent of normal children and is more common in children who experience night terrors. It usually occurs within two hours of bedtime and lasts about 15 minutes. Obviously, you need to seriously childproof your house if you have a little sleepwalker. Put a bell on his door so you can tell he is roaming.

Tip: Note how long it typically takes him to sleepwalk after he goes to sleep. Then wake him up 15 minutes *before* that time and keep him up for about 5 minutes.

Bunk beds

Older children like the idea of bunk beds, but usually they want to be in the top bunk. Unfortunately, even five-year-olds have been known to fall out of the top bunk.

Bed rails are particularly important. Make sure yours has rounded ends so bedclothes can't get caught as your child climbs down. Otherwise your child can literally get hung on the side of the bed. Also buy a ladder with treaded or padded steps.

To deal with the inevitable disputes, you might want to shake things up a bit by declaring, for example, that Tuesday is "doubles" night—that means both kids get to sleep together. It isn't fair that the older child should always get the top bunk.

Add 15 minutes to bedtime storytelling

In addition to the same old stories, create one of your own. You might want to make up a character and let that character have nightly adventures. (Remember the princess in the Arabian Nights story who told stories every night because the king threatened to execute her when she stopped telling her tale?) Sometimes the child could be the star or hero.

With multiple children, you should have multiple stories or even songs. I always had a song for each child. On occasion one child would ask for the other child's song. My chiropractor, who has three children, tells elaborate stories to her middle daughter. Since this child loves rainbows and trampolines, she often tells stories of little girls on trampolines who bounce so high they reach the rainbow.

TIP

3-6 YEARS: PRESCHOOLERS

Sleep talking

Many children talk in their sleep. It's perfectly natural. Often, it's just babbling, which although loud and animated, cannot be understood. It occurs in deep sleep, and there is absolutely no reason to wake the child up. You may be tempted, but do not ask, "What did you say?" Your child will not remember it in the morning.

Leave wake-up goodies

If you know your child wakes early, encourage him to play by himself. Do this by leaving a cardboard box full of toys and coloring books he can easily get to. Leave a nutritious snack on his play table to tide him over. Bring in the goodies after he has gone to sleep. This really gives him something to look forward to.

Read <u>Goodnight Moon</u>

There is something so universally soothing about this classic story, written in 1947 by Margaret Wise Brown ("Goodnight cow jumping over the moon...."), that it has been translated into other languages. The words almost magically make children of almost any age feel warm and fuzzy as soon as they hear them.

On a strictly personal note, one of my children's all-time favorites was another moon book—*See the Moon* by Robert Kraus (Windmill Books, 1980), which had the added bonus of being a glow-in-the-dark book.

Keep an "up" child down

There are other tips to keep your early riser down for a while. Keep shades and windows closed to keep out noise and light. Depending on just how early she rises, don't feed her immediately. In fact, don't feed her at all if you want her to lie back down. Snacking at 5 A.M. could raise her energy output to uncontrollable. You know your child best. If she is high-strung, avoid the early A.M. food offering. (See tip #302.)

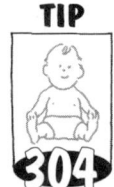

Day affects night

Understand that how well a child sleeps at night is often a barometer of how they are doing during the day. Daytime activities naturally affect nighttime. Let's say there's a change in the seasons and school is starting up again. Don't be surprised if you see variations in sleeping. So, if there is a sleep problem, think about what can be done during the day to make sleep easier. Maybe your children are overprogrammed when school starts up. They often show their stress by having difficulty with falling and staying asleep. You may cut back on after-school activities and see sleep problems disappearing as well. Or unwind before sleep by airing issues that came up during the day and are still haunting your little one.

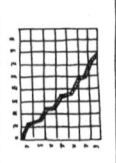

Review: Sleep milestones

Understand the turning points and milestones in your child's sleep patterns.

- 6 weeks—night sleep lengthens
- 12–16 weeks—daytime sleep regularizes
- 9 months—disappearance of night waking for feeding and the third nap
- 12–21 months—disappearance of morning nap
- 3–4 years—afternoon nap is less common

Thumb sucking, revisited

About 20 percent of children under five years old suck their thumbs. Thumb suckers are more likely to be attached to other objects like a lovey or a blanky. On the thumbs-up side, if your child sucks his thumb, he is more likely to sleep through the night. But when your mother chides you that this could affect his growing teeth, she has a point. But don't listen to suggestions that you discourage thumb sucking by wrapping the thumb in bandages or putting bitter solutions on it—the truth is these methods rarely work.

Usually the child does just grow out of it. But you can try to keep his thumbs busy during the day turning the pages of books and wrapped around stuffed animals at night.

Prepare for change

Prepare in advance when you know your child's schedule will be changed. For example, if you know your child is starting preschool on September 4 and has to be there at 8 A.M., don't wait until September 3. Begin in August to wake your child earlier in the morning. Slowly. Cheerfully. Happily. And simulate what you will be doing when school starts. Leave out clothes at night for her to get into in the morning—just as she will be doing. Or you might try to let her choose what she will wear on her first day. Change the nighttime ritual slightly—let her gather school supplies or add a stuffed animal to put in her Teletubby backpack.

TIP

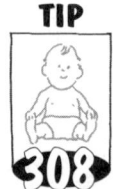

Naps, continued

Children three to six still nap, but *not every day*. Some children still need a nap or they need to go to bed earlier and sleep later. Your children are still going through transitions—like growth spurts—and changes in their schedules. Naps don't always fit in. But children still get tired.

Nap review	Frequency	Nap hours per day
4–6 months	2–3/day	3–7 hours
6–12 months	1–2/day	1–6 hours
2 years	1/day	1–3 hours
4 years	4/week	1–3 hours

"The sun will come out...tomorrow"

A great thing to do with a preschooler as you get ready for bed is to discuss plans for the following day. Tuck her in and say, "Go to sleep now and tomorrow when you get up we are going..." Again, this is a good time to help her wind down from her day. ("Let's say good night to your teacher." "Let's say good night to the bus driver.")

TIP 310

3-6 YEARS: PRESCHOOLERS

Why? Why? Why?

Preschoolers are notorious for asking a lot of questions—particularly to stall bedtime. Why is the sky blue? Why do people sneeze? (A new one I just heard in my office from a five-year-old: "When people lose weight, who finds it?") If you visit *www.amazon.com* and search for *Tell Me Why* you will find many adorable book choices to help you with this fun challenge.

Sleep instructions

If you are not going to be home, write down specific sleep instructions, including the sleep routine, for the baby-sitter or Grandma. There's a slight variation for older children. By preschool, your child knows there is a bigger world out there, and she can have her own special relationship with the baby-sitter or Grandma. Just make sure you and the babysitter are on the same page when it comes to nightime rituals.

Vacation time

If you are going on vacation, pack a stuffed animal, blanket, or some item the child is used to. You don't want to be scouring a strange neighborhood for a child's favorite item. I always encourage parents not to choose something too exotic—make sure it can easily be replicated. I once drove three hours back to a ski lodge to get my daughter's "Tibby." (Don't ask.) Kids can practically sniff out their special lovey. Never rely on having only one of these vital objects.

Bring along *anything* that plays an important role in your child's bedtime routine. It could be taped music or even favorite pj's.

Massage: "My turn"

By the time your child is a preschooler, you can massage his entire body and follow his lead. (He'll let you know what he likes.) Be firm in your strokes. Avoid tickling or you will wind him up and not down for sleep. You can offer massage as an incentive for him to get into his pj's and get ready for bed. This is a good age where you can massage each other. They usually want to do you first, so by the time it's their turn, you should be able to put them to sleep. (And feel relaxed as well.)

Children of divorce

The preschool child must have familiar things in the "other house"; that is, the place she visits, which is typically the father's house. I strongly recommend that you buy two sets of the same bedding, two of the same toothbrushes, even two sets of the same bedtime books. Try to be consistent. Ideally, the other parent will be sensitive to this issue and not oppositional. You can't take away all the pain, and children are always in some pain over the divorce, no matter how amicable it is, but you can help make bedtime more normal.

"Uh, where do I sleep?"

The child must not sleep in bed with the other parent—the one he is with less often. Children are in fact made more clinging and insecure in most cases where sleeping with one parent is allowed and sleeping with the other parent is not allowed. I feel really strongly that no matter what the economic circumstances, the child must have a specific space to sleep in that is just his. If you can't afford a bed, then get a futon. I have had teenagers complain to me bitterly that when they were little and slept over at their dad's house, they had to make do with sleeping on the couch in the living room. This makes the child feel like an intruder, a visitor, and not really welcome.

Divorce: Easing into bedtime

Encourage your child to check in at night with the *other* parent before bedtime. The child should be allowed to call the parent; just make sure this is at least half an hour before bedtime. Provide your child with a picture of the other parent as he travels between homes. Your being reassuring lets the child know it is okay to keep the other parent close to his heart at the other camp.

Divorce: Create a new ritual

Create a new sleep ritual that you share with your child. You can continue some of the ritual of the first home, but add something special and new that is just done at your home. This is particularly important if you were not actively involved in the bedtime ritual at the old homestead.

TIP

3-6 YEARS: PRESCHOOLERS

Travel: Sleep tips

When traveling, your child should not sleep with you if he doesn't at home, even if you have to put blankets on the floor or bring along a sleeping bag. This makes the trip more adventurous and you won't have to undo any bad habits after you return home. (When you get to the hotel, notify the front desk to hold calls after bedtime.)

Day-Glo stickers for nighttime

Day-Glo stars on the ceiling are a nice addition to a preschooler's room. You can view these glow-in-the-dark decals as an alternative to a night-light. If you don't want to turn his room into a planetarium, there are stickers in the shape of bugs, planes—you name it. Let him give input into what he wants decorating his ceiling. He is the one who sees it every night when he's lying down in bed.

3-6 YEARS: PRESCHOOLERS

Good morning/good-bye

A word about wake-ups: Never leave home in the morning without saying good-bye to your child, or she may not want to go to sleep at night. She may rise earlier and earlier just to catch you. She will be mad at you or afraid you will disappear again, if you are not there in the morning. (Sure, children can hold a grudge.) Even if you (mistakenly) thought your baby didn't notice if you came or went, your preschooler definitely will, and it's even more vital than ever that you not sneak out while she sleeps.

TIP

The first sleepover

Make sure your child really wants to go to the other child's house for a sleepover. Set a time for you to call before bedtime and in the morning. (A preschooler should be allowed to change her mind. She could get to her friend's house and decide it's too scary to stay. So make sure you are at home to get her goodnight call or her pick-me-up-now call.) Let your child take a stuffed animal or some favorite object. Let the host parent in on some important sleep rituals and, of course, any details, like bed-wetting behavior, that relate to sleep time.

TIP

Sleepover: Rehearsal

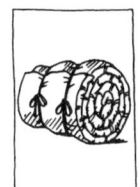

Just to be sure your child is ready, you can have a dress rehearsal, or in this case, a pj rehearsal. Have a pretend sleepover where everyone is dressed "down" for sleep, reads stories, stays up late, and then the invited sleepover guest gets to go home—with her parents! Another way to make sure your child is ready to sleep out is to do a test at a relative's house. Bring the child's favorite belongings and read her favorite story. Make it really fun to be at Auntie Jane's house. (Obviously, if your child fusses at Auntie Jane's, then she "flunks" and needs a little more time.)

Guess who's sleeping over

If your child is the "resident" child, encourage your child to share, but he doesn't have to share his bedtime story. Tell two stories that night. Maybe even three—one for each child and one for the duo. Nighttime is disorienting, more so at a new place. Make sure you leave a nightlight on.

When a friend sleeps over for the first time, practice getting him to the bathroom. You might even try marking the route to the bathroom with glow tape for fun. And leave the bathroom light on as well.

Fever

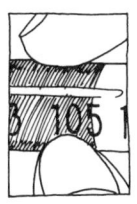

If your child has a fever during the day, treat appropriately with a children's version of fever medicine. But do *not* wake the child during the night to give more fever medicine or to take her temperature. If she is sleeping, then she is not uncomfortable and should be left asleep. This one is really tough for parents who are always calling me to ask how often they should take their child's temperature. I say, "As little as possible." If your child is hot at night, she is in no more danger than being hot during the day. Except for very young infants, most fever is not dangerous.

Bed-wetting: The facts

First some facts: Five million children over the age of six still wet their bed. Of that group, as they get older, they stop at the rate of 10 percent a year. By the time most kids reach adolescence they are no longer bed-wetting. Let me make this really clear: Most *parents* have a problem with bed-wetting, not children. I see it as a laundry issue, not a sleep one.

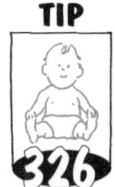

Bed-wetting and sleeping

The truth is that most children who wet their bed sleep very deeply. The sleep problem occurs as a result of parents manipulating the child. Parents, in a misguided attempt to teach the child not to wet the bed, often wake the child up. All this does is create sleep problems. Remember the crucial rule: *Never wake a sleeping child.* Do not wake the child at 11 P.M. to empty his bladder. (But you could limit fluids after dinner.) Let him sleep. Nothing worse should happen to your child than to have a little rash from lying in pee overnight.

The wet bed

Some parents really can't stand the notion of the child in a wet bed. A simple solution for parents who can't control themselves is to use triple sheeting. Here's what works: Put on a layer of plastic/sheet, plastic/sheet, plastic/sheet. Children who bed-wet, often do so more than once a night. This way, if you have a compulsion to keep the bed dry, you just gently roll the child over to one side, pull off one set of sheets at a time, and roll him back.

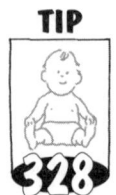

Bed-wetting: Dressing for success

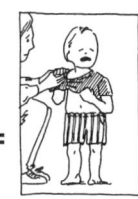

You can dress your child for easier access if you have to change him. For those children who do wet the bed and then get up, have them wear T-shirts, not one-piece footed pajamas or tops and bottoms. It's easier to slip a big T-shirt off and put on a dry one. Also, put a larger child in large-size Pull-ups or even Depends.

No punishment

Your child cannot help bed-wetting. Don't ever punish him—that is just adding insult to the injury. Humiliation breeds deception and poor self-image. Some children are so afraid of the consequences of bed-wetting, they try not to go to sleep at all. Then they are overtired during the day, and it just breeds more sleeping problems.

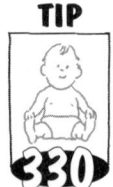

The medicine cabinet for preschoolers

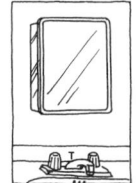

Make sure you know child's weight for correct dosage.

- painkillers—acetaminophen/ibuprofen (both for fever, the latter for pain)
- teething gel—great for toothaches of all sorts
- antacid for tummy aches, like children's Mylanta or other calcium carbonate preparation
- ear drops for pain
- saline drops for simple stuffy noses—nasal spray for emergencies only
- neosynephrine or pseudo-ephedrine for ear pain emergencies only, but call your doctor first
- cold medication, previously tested so you know what side effects to expect

Just say no... to a thermometer at night

It is rarely necessary to take a preschooler's temperature in the middle of the night. (See tip #325, "Fever.") At this age, it is practically torture to use a thermometer to see if the child has a fever. If you are not sure (which is what parents tell me), then the truth is she probably does not have a fever. If she has a fever during the day, then treat. Otherwise, *never wake a child just to take her temperature.* If she is fast asleep, that is what her body needs.

Stuffed animals stand guard!

"When my son was three we had a new baby in the house and he started getting up again at night worried about monsters. So I stationed a huge stuffed monkey down the hall to guard him. I placed it so he could see it from his bed. In addition, just to be really 'safe,' I put stuffed animals right outside his door for his 'protection.' It worked!"

TIP

3-6 YEARS: PRESCHOOLERS

Colds and the preschooler

Encourage your sick child to drink lots of very warm liquids during the day. If she doesn't like her beverage hot, you can drop an ice cube into it or make a nice herbal tea and let her *inhale* the aroma. This helps clear the sinuses and soothes the chest. At this age she can tolerate five-minute intervals in a steamy bathroom with the lights turned low and soothing music. This can be coupled with a eucalyptus or camphor-based rub—just be sure to keep it out of your child's reach. Seat your child on your lap and gently sway. She might enjoy the company of a toy or stuffed animal.

Treating a stuffed nose

At this age you can use Vicks Vapo rub. Yes, it's been around forever—because it works. Saline nose drops can help clear a child's nose. You can even make your own: Just add a quarter teaspoon of salt to four ounces of water and drip it in with a dropper. The number of drops is unimportant, but don't use any device to suction the drops back out. Nasal sprays can also be useful. Some young children can't or won't sniff in, so it's easier to use a spray instead of drops. Often even preschoolers won't lie down to let drops be absorbed. So use spray and be quick about it. "Squirt. Squirt. All done."

TIP

Teeth grinding

Some children grind their teeth at night. Despite what your aunt or neighbor told you, it is not a sign of stress in young children. It is not necessary to wake your child. She may level down some of her teeth, but usually it is insignificant, and she'll get another set of teeth anyway. Just live with it. (*Tip:* Sometimes just changing the pillow helps.)

Earaches

Ask your doctor for a prescription for anesthetic ear drops "just in case" and use liberally with a child who wakes up with an earache. It's easier to have a dropper filled and ready than to have to start heating up oil. (See tip #257.) But the same rules apply as for oil: Do not use if child has any ear discharge. (Also, for preschoolers, one squirt in each nostril of neosynephrine.) Try having him lie on a heating pad, or a warm water bottle under a pillowcase. *Warning:* Don't use a heating pad for a child who wets the bed; use a hot water bottle instead.

Last words of the evening

Make the last words you say to your child each night very special. Use some variation of "I love you," or create your own warm and fuzzy last words. One mother would rub her son's temples and say: "In with the good dreams, out with the bad, in with the happy dreams, out with the sad." If your child is on a sleepover, or you are on a trip, you can prearrange a time when you will silently send out the good dreams. Don't be surprised if your child checks up on you and asks if you sent out good dreams when you said you would.

Never say goodnight in anger

Sometimes, despite your best efforts, you may be angry with your child and say goodnight abruptly or even angrily. I urge you to go back in the room, even if your child has sort of fallen asleep. It's better to risk a slight disruption than to let your child's last image of you be a hostile one. Once, a relative *instructed* me to go back to my son when I was in this position. When I said, "But he's asleep," he replied, "He'll know you are there." I went back in and whispered in my son's ear and his arm came up to touch me.

Avoid junk foods close to bedtime

Foods high in sugar may interfere with sleep by raising your child's energy level. A high-sugar meal can trigger the body to produce excessive insulin, which causes the blood sugar to fall rapidly to low levels during the night. This can disturb sleep.

Parent-to-parent: Rub the third eye

"My Aunt swears by this one. She gently rubs the space between her child's eyes in a clock-ways motion to calm her. She is from Indonesia, but I'm not sure if that is a cultural thing."

Parent-to-parent: Rub eyebrows

"I have one that always worked for our kids. While they are lying down, but will not yet give in to sleep, no matter how tired, I gently rub their eyebrows with my fingers. I do this one eyebrow at a time. Usually they are on their side, so whatever side is 'up' I do first. It works really fast, and off they go to dreamland."

3-6 YEARS: PRESCHOOLERS

Parent-to-parent: Stroke lightly

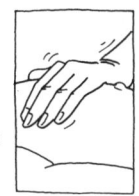

"When I was little, my mom used to stroke our arms, hands, and faces lightly with her fingernails. It was so relaxing. To this day when I can't sleep, I have my daughter do the same thing to me."

Read <u>I Don't Want to Sleep Tonight</u>

This is a delightful pop-up book written by the television personality and mother of three, Deborah Norville. *I Don't Want to Sleep Tonight* (Golden Books, 1999) specifically addresses the issue of children having scary dreams after watching television or playing video games close to bedtime. ("I don't want to sleep tonight, There's a monster in my room, He waits until the lights go out, And fills the room with gloom.")

TIP 344

3-6 YEARS: PRESCHOOLERS

Parent-to-parent: Ending a night terror

"A lot of parents don't know what to do about night terrors and feel really frustrated. In one parent group, it was suggested that you take the child into the bathroom and place her feet in cold water. I have absolutely no idea why this might work, but several parents have used this method and claim it ends that particular episode. I guess the child just wakes up!"

TIP

3-6 YEARS: PRESCHOOLERS

The bedtime pass

Give your child a "bedtime pass" entitling him to "get out of bed free" one time. The *Archives of Pediatrics and Adolescent Medicine* recently reported on "The Bed Time Pass." In their study, in every case, children would exchange their pass for a one-time simple request and then would go back to sleep because they had no more passes. It gives children some control over their lives and the "logic" of the pass seems to appeal to them.

The night after a vaccine

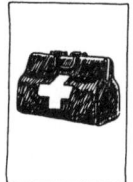

For any age child, the night after receiving a vaccine can present problems whether because of the material in the vaccine or because of the hurt from the injection. Your child may get up and cry. Always go in and check on a child who has had a vaccine, both for safety and for emotional support. You are looking for any reaction at the site of the injection or an allergic reaction like a rash. Then all bets are off, and call your pediatrician.

TIP

The night after a trauma

Kids routinely fall and have accidents and get boo-boos. A few days ago, one of my little patients was sitting in her stroller when a car hit it. Fortunately, only the stroller got bent. The child was physically just fine, but she has not slept through the night since. She screams. If you know your child has had a day of trauma, talk to her, even if she is preverbal, before bedtime. "I know what happened to you today. You are safe now. Daddy is right here." Go into the room briefly to check for signs of distress for at least a night or two.

The hospital experience

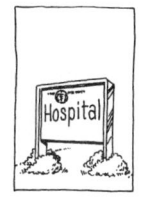

A child who has been hospitalized may have sleep difficulties when he comes home. Give a generous dose of daytime TLC. He needs to be touched, hugged, and kissed. Review with him what the day or days were like in the hospital. It should go without saying that if a child is in the hospital, a parent must spend the night with him. Period.

The magic disc

I was recently in a store called the Store of Knowledge. I found a disc that looked like it was manufactured in the Twilight Zone. It promised to help hypnotize a child to sleep through a series of whirling holograms. It sticks to the ceiling—right next to the Day-Glo stars. If you go into any magic shop, you will probably find some gadget that promises to hypnotize and/or put a child to sleep.

3-6 YEARS: PRESCHOOLERS

Family bed, revisited

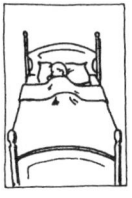

I'm often asked if it's okay if older preschoolers be allowed to sleep with their parents if they wake up in the middle of the night. It might seem like a warm and cuddly thing to do, but the family bed is a hard habit to break. Make this a lifestyle decision. By the time your child is a preschooler, she really is entitled to some privacy of her own, as are you. Again, if a child is scared or not feeling well, you can go into her room and keep her company. If there is a new baby in the house who is now in your bed, make sleeping in her own room really special for your preschooler—maybe Daddy goes in and lies down with her—briefly.

Just say no...to snoring

Your child shouldn't snore. If your child snores when he doesn't have a cold, you should consult your pediatrician. It's possibly a sign of a sleep disorder like obstructive sleep apnea (OSA). If your child doesn't wake up when he snores, you might think he doesn't have a sleep problem, but it still needs to be checked out. Your child's sleep might in fact be unhealthy and inefficient.

FYI: Children who snore are more likely to fall asleep during the day and be restless sleepers at night. They are also more likely to start bed-wetting. So the five-year-old who just starts snoring should really be checked out.

Read <u>Where the Wild Things Are</u>

Where the Wild Things Are, by Maurice Sendak (HarperCollins, 1963), is the award-winning tale of a mischievous boy who is sent to bed without his supper and sails into a wild nature adventure. Although *I* find this one a bit scary, it is a favorite with children of all ages.

Hotlines

The hotlines can provide some useful advice to parents.

1-800-NO SLEEP
1-800-583-4135—The National Parent Information Network

Magazines

Parents
Working Mother
Sesame Street Parents
American Baby
Parenting
Child

Sleep is a very popular subject and is often included in the so-called women's magazines. They're also fairly cheap, so get yourself a subscription.

TIP

Web sites

Here are some helpful online resources which provide information on a wide variety of topics.

> *www.drpaula.com* (The only site that gives you access to pediatricians.)
> *www.familyhealth.com*
> *www.parents.com*
> *www.parentsoup.com*

All will link you up to even more sites. And some have chat rooms where you can post questions and get answers back from other parents.

Sleep problems

Sometimes a child's sleep problems are not simple. There are so-called sleep disorders. Children who suffer from true sleep disorders are resistant to all your (365) efforts and have anxiety around sleep time and/or sleep very few hours. These may well be tomorrow's insomniacs. First, check with your regular pediatrician, then a neurologist, and then a sleep disorder clinic or center.

Read The Sleep Book for Tired Parents

An often overlooked problem with children struggling with sleep disorders is the effect a child's sleep disorder has on the entire family. This book, *The Sleep Book for Tired Parents,* by Rebecca Huntley (Parenting Press, 1991), helps to improve the quality of life for the entire family—sleepless child and all.

3-6 YEARS: PRESCHOOLERS

Signs of sleep disorders

Signs of sleep disorders include: Persistent night terrors or nightmares; periodic leg movement—also known as restless leg syndrome; or chronic insomnia, that is a child who really is up all night long. These conditions can significantly interfere with your child's development, impair growth, and affect school performance.

Sleep-disorder clinics, and more

Check out The American Sleep Disorders Association, a Web site that lists accredited sleep-disorder clinics nationwide. There are some sleep-disorder clinics that are affiliated with children's hospitals that may also be helpful. Searle Healthnet is a site that posts up-to-the-minute sleep research such as studies involving melatonin. Also check out Sleepnet, a clearinghouse site, and The Sleep Page, which links a huge number of potential resources. And then there are some specific organizations like The National Enuresis Society for children who wet the bed (7777 Forest Lane, Dallas, TX, 75230) and the Restless Legs Syndrome Foundation (4410 19th Street NW, Rochester, MN, 55901). In other words, there's probably some organization out there that can help with almost any sleep problem!

Sing "Waltzing Matilda"

I've included this lovely waltz even though none of my friends are Australian.

Oh, there once was a swagman camped in the billabong,
Under the shade of a coolibah tree,
And he sang as he looked at the old billy boiled
"Who'll come a-waltzing Matilda with me"

Who'll come a-waltzing Matilda my darling,
Who'll come a-waltzing Matilda with me?
Waltzing Matilda and leading a waterbag,
Who'll come a-waltzing Matilda with me?

Down came the jumbuck to drink at the water-hole,
Up jumped the swagman and grabbed him with glee,
And he sang as he put him away in his tucker-bag,
"You'll come a-waltzing, Matilda with me."

Up came the squatter, a-riding his thoroughbred,
Up came policemen—one, two and three
Whose is that jumpbuck you've got in the tucker-bag,
You'll come a-waltzing Matilda with me.

The swagman he up and he jumped in the water-hole,
Drowning himself by the coolibah tree,
And his ghost may be heard as it sings by the billabong,
Who'll come a-waltzing Matilda with me?

3-6 YEARS: PRESCHOOLERS

Lullabies online

Can't sing "Lullaby and Goodnight" one more time? Running out of ideas? Go surfing, online. One good site is "KIDiddles Online Store" at *www.kiddles.com/shop2babies*. It lists music for babies and toddlers and takes you browsing through listings of lullabies and bedtime stories. It even lists sheet music.

Sleep affects behavior

Exhausted kids are more likely to be cranky and impatient and do poorly in school. Children who don't get a minimum number of the required hours of sleep, which does vary, are more likely to be irritable and have poor attention spans and slower reaction times. Conversely, sleep can be a "cure" for a child who is fidgety or not doing well in school.

TIP

Waking up in the middle of the night can be a good sign!

According to world-renowned pediatrician T. Berry Brazelton, whom I had the pleasure of meeting once as my surprise birthday present, there may be a good explanation for occasional periods of sleep difficulties. He hypothesizes these periods are sometimes related to children's growth and development. The child may be up at night while he thinks, processes, catches up to a new skill he is in the midst of acquiring—walking, crawling, climbing. As teenagers like to say: "It's all good." So notice if your child's wakefulness is connected to acquiring some new skill. Celebrate. It will pass.

The last word

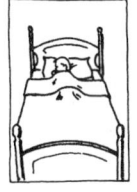

You will eventually get a child who not only sleeps through the night, but also sleeps for long periods of time. It's called a teenager. Be careful what you wish for! Teens are notorious for their sleeping habits. So yes, eventually, you will not be sleep deprived. Except when you are waiting for your teen to return home—with your car.